EFFECTIVE TEAMWORKING: reducing the psychosocial risks

Dr Sharon K Parker BSc (Hons), PhD
and Dr Helen M Williams BSc (Hons), PhD
Institute of Work Psychology
University of Sheffield
Sheffield
S10 2TN

Case studies in practitioner format

HSE BOOKS

First published 2001

ISBN 0 7176 2149 9

The Institute of Work Psychology

The Institute of Work Psychology, established by the University of Sheffield in 1994, is staffed by research scientists and support staff, with a large group of postgraduate students (masters and doctoral). The Institute of Work Psychology is dedicated to conducting applied research in work settings with the aim of advancing knowledge about the factors that influence individual, team and organisational well-being and effectiveness.

CONTENTS

GUIDE TO THE REPORT

The abstract provides an overview of the main findings of this report.

Section 1 is an executive summary of the report that is intended for those who do not have time to read the full report.

Section 2 outlines the background to the research.

Section 3 identifies team working as a prevalent form of work organisation flexibility. To set team working within a wider context, the different types of flexibility that can occur within organisations (i.e., functional, financial, geographic, and work organisation flexibility) are also described.

Section 4 describes team working in more detail, including what team working is, different types of team working, leadership models for team working, and definitions of what is an effective team. This section is therefore useful for people who are thinking about implementing team working within their organisation since it outlines the basic elements of team working and the choices that need to be made.

Section 5 describes theoretical perspectives relevant to team working, including the Job Characteristics Model, Socio-technical Systems Theory, and Input-Process-Output Models of team effectiveness. This section is useful for those who want to gain a deeper understanding of the philosophy behind different types of team working.

Section 6 describes existing academic literature on the effect of team working on employee mental health, as well as its impact on organisational outcomes such as performance. This section is therefore useful for those who want to learn about the progress that academics have made in understanding the impact that team working can have on employees and organisations.

Section 7 proposes a model to enhance understanding of team working and its effects on employee well being. The model proposes several ways that organisations can maximise the positive effects of team working for employee's mental health and ways in which organisations can minimise its risks for work-related stress. The findings from the studies conducted as part of this research are integrated into this discussion. This section is therefore useful to those who want to implement team working, since it provides guidance as to how to increase the likelihood of a successful team working initiative. It also offers some conclusions and recommendations regarding the effect of team working on employee mental health.

The final three sections present the findings of the current research studies in a case-study format to facilitate dissemination to practitioners. Section 8 describes a follow-up of the implementation of team working within a brown-field wire-manufacturing site. Section 9 discusses a case in which lean production cells were introduced in a vehicle manufacturing plant. Finally, section 10 describes the transition between traditional team working and self-managed team working within a chemical processing plant.

1. EXECUTIVE SUMMARY

Work-related stress is an important national issue. At the same time, vast change is occurring within the modern work place that has the potential to escalate work-related stress.

This report focuses on team working, which is an increasingly prevalent trend. On the one hand, team working might be a way of way of *reducing work-related stress*, such as through enhancing employees' job autonomy. On the other hand, there is a danger that flexible work practices such as team working could *escalate employee stress levels*, such as through increasing work pressure. It is therefore important to understand how the positive effects of team working can be enhanced whilst the negative effects can be minimised or prevented.

The current research aimed to report on existing team working research in relation to employee mental health, as well as to report on the results of three studies conducted by the authors:

- Study 1: A longitudinal study of the effects of implementing *flexible work teams* in a wire-making company
- Study 2: A longitudinal study of *lean production teams* in a vehicle manufacturing company
- Study 3: An investigation of *self-managed teams* in a chemical processing company

This executive summary provides a practitioner-oriented summary of the final report. Links to the more detailed sections of the report are indicated where relevant.

Why study team working?

Team working is an increasingly popular way of achieving greater organisational flexibility, as well as other benefits such as reduced costs of supervision, faster lead times, innovation, more effective decision-making, better customer service, and enhanced employee morale. In the mid-1990's, 55% of UK manufacturing companies reported using team working. This usage of team working is predicted to grow, even more so than other flexible production initiatives *(see Section 3.2 for more detail on this aspect)*.

What is team working and what is an effective team?

A team is more than a group of people working near to each other. Defining features of a team include:

- a team has a defined organisational function and identity (i.e., the team has a specific task or set of tasks to perform)
- a team has shared objectives or goals
- the team members must have interdependent roles (i.e., the members need to co-ordinate with each other to get the work done)

An *effective* team is more than simply a team that performs well in the short term. Typically, an effective team is considered to be one that performs well *and* that has team members who are satisfied and not stressed, has low turnover and absence, and that is viable (i.e., sustainable). These multiple criteria should be used when assessing the success of team working. *(See Sections 4.1 and 4.2 for more detail on what is a team and an effective team).*

Are all teams the same?

There are many different forms of team working, and it is important to distinguish between them when investigating their consequences. The teams we focus on in our research are:

- teams that produce goods or services (rather than teams that process information)
- teams that are permanent structures (rather than that are created on a temporary basis to solve a particular problem, such as software development teams)
- teams that involve members working as a team to carry out their core tasks (rather than team activities carried out off the job, such as quality circles).

Although we are focusing on relatively permanent teams that carry out core work tasks to produce goods and services, these teams still vary in quite fundamental ways. They vary according to the following:

- **the degree of team member autonomy and involvement in decision-making** (e.g., some teams are themselves responsible for the day-to-day running of the teams, whereas other teams have little autonomy over decisions)
- **the scope of involvement** (e.g., some teams are involved in activities such as recruiting and disciplining team members, whereas other teams are only involved in production work)

- **type of team leadership** (e.g., some teams have a tightly-controlling supervisor, some have a 'hands-on' team leader who works as part of the team, and some teams manage themselves)
- **degree of standardisation of procedures within teams** (e.g., some teams have highly standardised methods for their core tasks whereas others decide their own methods)

In this research, we focused on four types of teams that arise from combinations of the above characteristics *(see Section 3.3.3 for more detail)*:

- **Traditional work groups**

  These are controlled by a first line supervisor, have a low degree of involvement and a low scope of involvement. They are also often not 'teams' in the sense that they have low task interdependence and do not possess shared work goals.
- **Lean production teams**

  These are characterised by the standard operating procedures that regulate team members' work. Typically there is a first line supervisor who manages the team, and often there are off-line continuous improvement activities. The work of lean production teams is heavily production-focused with little employee involvement in management or support activities, and a low scope of involvement.
- **Flexible work teams**

  Flexible work teams have a greater degree and scope of involvement than traditional work groups, but they do not have as much involvement or autonomy as self-managing teams. They are usually led by a 'hands on' team leader, or a team member that works within the team but also has a role in the running of the team.
- **Self-managed teams.**

  These teams have a high degree of involvement. Team members have responsibility for the performance of the team and the autonomy to make decisions regarding issues such as the methods of working, assigning members to tasks, solving production and interpersonal problems, and conducting meetings. Typically, self-managing teams are led by external managers who act as facilitators and managers of the boundary between the team and others, rather than as supervisors who closely direct the team's activities.

It is important that those contemplating introducing teams are aware of the ways in which teams can vary as different types of teams can have different consequences for employees' mental health.

What is the effect of team working on employees?

Several studies have investigated the effects of team working on outcomes such as employee motivation, employee job satisfaction and employee stress *(see Section 5 for more detail)*. Unfortunately, many of the studies are not rigorous in research terms, and their conclusions cannot be relied upon. Nevertheless , from the few rigorous studies that exist (e.g., those with longitudinal research designs), the evidence suggests that team working can enhance employees' job satisfaction and their level of commitment to the organisation. The likelihood of positive consequences for employees is particularly high for *self-managing teams,* which have high levels of employee involvement and autonomy.

Research has also shown that teams, especially self-managing teams, can lead to better performance and productivity (e.g., greater sales, improved quality, reduced absence). However, positive benefits have not been reported in all cases.

One type of team however, stands out from this general picture. This is the *lean production team,* in which team members' work on tightly-linked tasks that have highly standardised methods. Some commentators have criticised lean production teams for being 'mean' teams because they remove individual discretion and increase work load, whereas others suggest that because employees rotate jobs and share responsibilities, job quality is enhanced as a result of lean production. Of the small number of studies that have investigated lean production teams, the findings are contradictory. A recent review of studies erred on the side of concluding that lean production has negative consequences for employees; that is, lean production intensifies work demands and work pace, with increases in decision-making authority and skill levels being very modest and/or temporary. The author of this review however, acknowledged that this conclusion is limited by the lack of well-designed studies on the topic. Study 2 reports an investigation of lean production teams.

How do organisations maximise potential effects of team working for employees? And minimise negative effects?

Existing research, and our own studies, have shown that team working can promote employee well-being at work and can, in some cases, increase organisational effectiveness. However, the beneficial effects are not as great or as consistent as we would expect from the theory, particularly when it comes to enhancing organisational performance. There is also less evidence for positive effects of lean production teams; indeed there is evidence suggesting negative effects.

We propose a model that will enhance understanding of why, when and how team working has a positive impact on effectiveness, especially employee well-being *(see Section 6 for more details).* The key propositions that arise from model are elaborated below:

- **Proposition 1: Enriched work design will enhance employee well-being, as long as excess demands are not placed upon team members**

  This first proposition is not particularly new, and derives from a large body of research concerning the link between work characteristics and well-being. Essentially, the more that a job is designed to have enriching work characteristics, such as job autonomy and skill variety, then the more likely that employees will be satisfied, motivated, and mentally healthy. Because aspects such as high work load and role conflict can cause strain, efforts should be made to ensure these work characteristics are monitored to ensure they do not escalate to damaging levels.

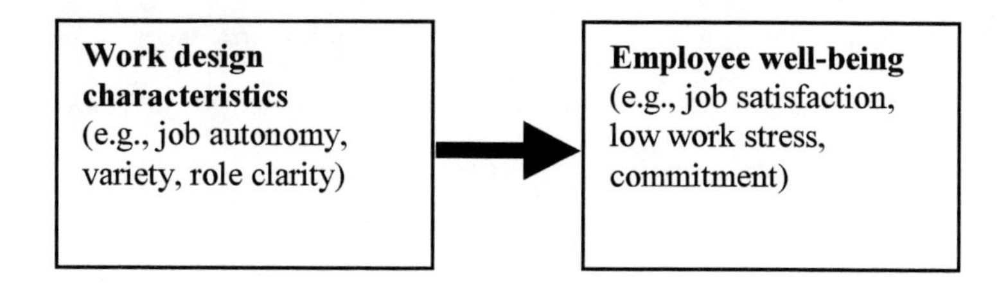

Some important work design characteristics for employee well-being that have been identified in the research are described below. Essentially, the presence of these work characteristics makes for an 'enriched job':

- job autonomy/decision-making authority
- a lack of job pacing
- skill variety and opportunity to develop new skills
- feedback about performance
- carrying out a whole task and a meaningful job
- reasonable levels of work load demands
- clear goals (role clarity)
- consistency in what is expected (absence of role conflict)
- positive relationships with colleagues

- **Proposition 2: The effect of team working on employee well-being will depend on how team working affects work design characteristics**

  Based on Proposition 1, it follows that the effect of team working on employees will depend on how the team working initiative affects work characteristics:

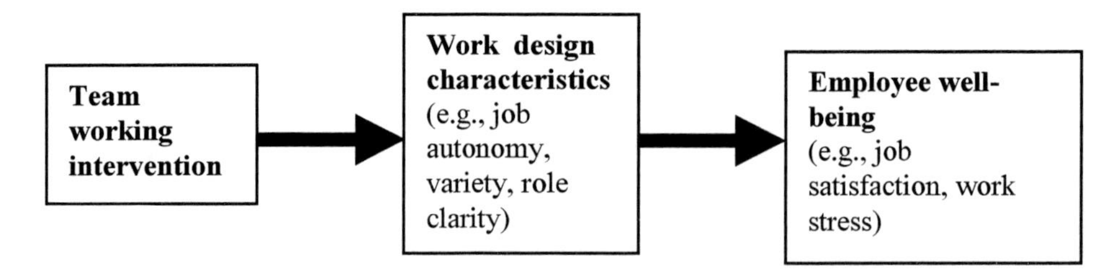

For example, if team working *enhances* enriching work characteristics such as job control and task variety, and does not have any other negative effects, then team working should lead to greater job satisfaction and lower work-related stress. However, if team working *diminishes* work characteristics such as job control, then it is likely to have a negative effect. Similarly, if team working increases stressful aspects of work (such as by increasing employees' work load to unreasonable levels), without compensatory positive consequences for jobs, it will be associated with more stress.

Our research in this project clearly shows that where team working has had a positive effect on work characteristics (e.g., resulting in enhanced team member autonomy), then there were benefits for team well-being.

For example, Study 2 describes a situation in which teams were introduced within some areas of production. The teams involved groups working together to standardise their work procedures, and therefore represent an early form of *lean production teams*. The only teams where there was some positive mental health benefit were those where team activities were supported, and where team members had influence over decision-making. Where teams were introduced in a way that did not allow for employee participation, and where the team activities were not supported by others, then the lean teams had negative effects for employee well-being *(see Study 2, Section 8 for more detail of this finding).*

What this means in practical terms is that **if organisations want to ensure team working is positive for employees, they need to design and implement teams such that they will have a positive impact on work characteristics.** Next, we consider some of the ways that organisations can act to maximise the likelihood of this outcome.

- **Proposition 3: The effect of team working on work characteristics depends on the appropriateness of the context for team working, the design of team working, and how well it is implemented.**

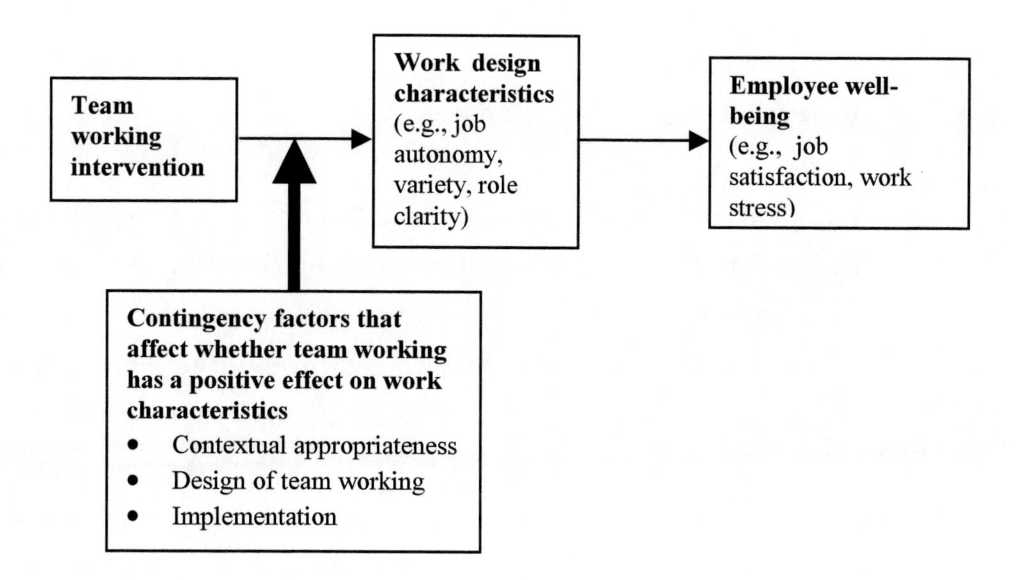

The point here is that, by paying attention to the following factors, managers can increase the likelihood that team working will have positive effects on employees' jobs and hence their well-being. Factors that affect the success of team working are described next *(see Section 6.3 for more detail):*

- **Introducing team working in an appropriate context**

  Sometimes team working is introduced in organisations because it is 'the thing to do', such as because competitors have team working. However, team working should only be introduced if it is appropriate for the organisational context. By an appropriate organisational context, we mean that at least two conditions should hold:

  (i) *there should be some degree of interdependence.* In other words, there should be some need for employees to co-operate and collaborate to achieve the team goals. If interdependence is low, and employees do not need to work together to achieve their goals, the value of team working is likely to be lower, and could even be detrimental.

  For example, in Study 1, there was one area of the company where team working was found not to exist despite having been 'implemented'. A detailed examination showed that, not only were the teams spread over such a large area that working together was very difficult, but the team members did not need each other in order to get their job done. If team members did help their team mates, their own productivity was likely to be reduced because they could not simultaneously watch their own machine. After the failed implementation, the employees in this area were more stressed than they had been prior to the initiative *(see Study 1, Section 7 for a detailed description of this finding).*

We recommend that companies establish whether there is any interdependence amongst tasks before implementing team working. If there is little interdependence (i.e., not much value in team member co-operation), then team working should not be implemented at this stage. Instead, one alternative is to *enrich individual jobs*, such as through job enrichment schemes (e.g., allow employees to carry out their own preventative maintenance). Another option is that organisations can explicitly seek to *increase the interdependence* between the tasks prior to introducing team working, such as by introducing cellular manufacturing (i.e., the grouping of machines, people, and processes into 'cells' where a particular product or type of product is made) or introducing shared goals that explicitly require co-ordination across the team.

(ii) *the organisation should be 'ready' for team working.* If the structure and culture of the organisation are highly bureaucratised (as in many traditional companies), then the implementation of a team-based structure, especially a self-managing team structure, is likely to be fraught with difficulty. The organisation's culture, structure and systems should be 'ready' for team working. Here are some examples of 'readiness':

- employees should be able to suggest and implement improvements to their work area without going through several levels of approval
- the technology should be flexible enough to permit restructuring or reorganisation based on the needs of the teams
- management in the organisation should be willing to adjust responsibility downwards and radically change their own roles and behaviour

In large part, the lack of 'organisational readiness' for team working was a reason that it was not successful within the production area described in Study 1. The organisation had a strong culture of hierarchical decision-making and managerial control, which was not conducive to team working *(see Study 1, Section 7).*

- **An appropriate design for team working**

When organisations embark on team working, there are several decisions that need to be made regarding the design and model of team working. These include:

(i) *size and scope of the team.* A team should constitute a 'logical' task grouping, in which there is a clear boundary between the group's work and the work of others. The team should also have clear shared goals that cover a number of aspects (e.g., customer satisfaction, quality, efficiency). The team should usually involve a manageable number of people (10-12 is usually considered the upper limit). Study 2 shows how larger-sized teams (some with as many as 20 people) were less effective than smaller-sized teams *(see Section 8).*

(ii) degree of employee self-management in the team. A self-managing team design is the most likely to result in enhanced employee well-being, especially if the environment is a complex one involving high uncertainty. Based on socio-technical systems theory, a recommendation is that the team should have sufficient autonomy to plan and manage all aspects of their own work. This includes responsibility for the following types of activities:

- setting goals, planning and scheduling
- allocating work amongst group members
- deciding on work methods
- obtaining and evaluating measures of work performance
- selecting and training group members

Study 2 describes the introduction of lean production teams, which by virtue of their focus on standardised processes, are unlikely to enhance job autonomy and might even decrease it. Therefore, organisations contemplating the introduction of team working need to be made aware that there are different models of team working, and that the model they choose could dramatically affect team working's success and its impact on employee well-being.

(iii) *models of supervision.* An important aspect relating to the model of team working concerns the choices made regarding the style and structure of supervision. One problem with retaining traditional supervisors is that they are often reluctant to relinquish control to team members, which results in teams not having the autonomy that they need to solve problems effectively. This problem can also occur with 'team leaders'.

This was illustrated in Study 3, which showed that one of the main barriers to the development of self-managed team working, was managers' taking a 'controlling' supervision style. In order for self-managed teams to actually organise their own work, managers need to relinquish decision-making to the teams.

Study 3 also showed that the full benefits of self-managing team working can only be achieved if a large number of team members take on self-managing responsibilities. When just one or two members take most responsibility, the effects of the implementation of team working were less beneficial.

A key role of someone who manages a self-managing team will be 'boundary management', in which the individual liaises with other team and other departments to ensure the group has the necessary resources. Managers typically need training in this role.

- **Implementation factors**

Having designed an appropriate team work design, team working then needs to be implemented. Some important factors for the successful implementation of team working are described next *(see Section 6.3.4 for more detail):*

(i) *a clear strategy for implementing team working that is widely disseminated*

(ii) *management commitment to team working.* For example, one of the major differentiating factors that explained the relative success of team working in maintenance compared to production (Study 1) was management commitment.

(iii) *realistic expectations and a long-term approach to team working implementation.* For example, in one part of the company (production) described in Study 1, teams were implemented, but thereafter there was little or no emphasis by managers on team working. However, in another part of the company (maintenance), managers spent considerable time and effort developing the teams and seeking ways to improve team working. Although both areas saw benefits of team working in the short term, in the long term only those teams that had been continually developed were still successfully operating in teams.

(iv) *sufficient resources allocated to team working, especially for training.* For example, in Study 2, insufficient *time resources* were given to responding to lean time activities and requests. To progress their ideas for improvement, team members needed the support of other departments and personnel to make the changes happen. For example, the purchasing department needed to approve various decisions. However, this support and assistance was often not forthcoming, which was de-motivating for team members.

(v) *stakeholder involvement and participation in the design and implementation process.*

(vi) *Alignment of wider organisational and human resource systems with team working, including the following:*

- *flexible and broad job descriptions*
- *reward/grading system that promote appropriate behaviours (e.g., team-based pay)*
- *systems to monitor and facilitate training*
- *the availability of non-hierarchical career paths*
- *recruitment and selection systems based on appropriate criteria (e.g., preference for group working, trainability)*
- *clear performance criteria/targets for the team*
- *feedback and information systems that allow the team to act on problems that arise, make appropriate decisions, interact with other groups, and learn from their mistakes*
- *layout of the work environment conductive to team working (team members near each other and somewhat separate from other teams)*
- *modifications to technology to support enriched work roles*

Proposition 4: The effect of work design characteristics on well-being outcomes depends on various individual and contextual factors

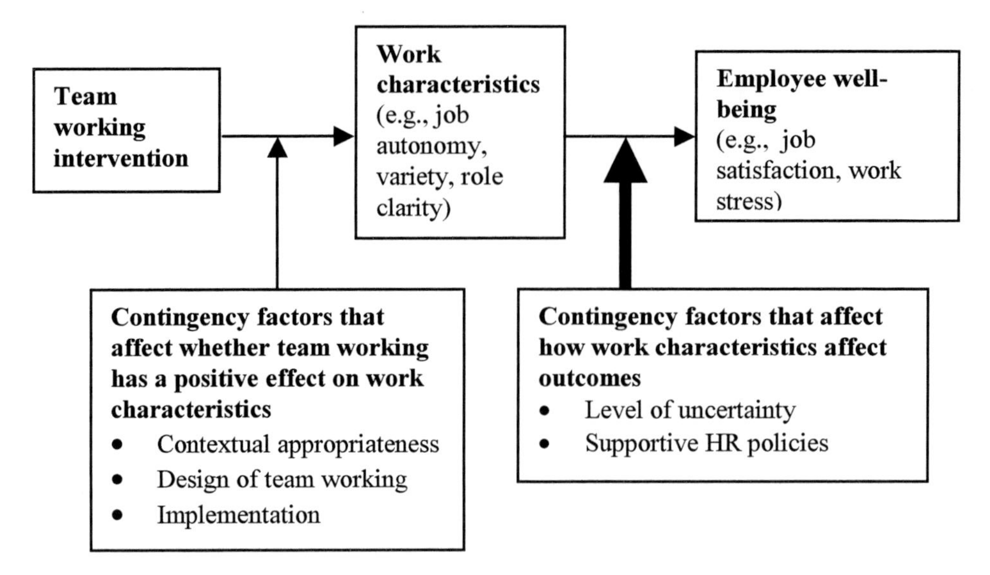

The final point to make is that there are some 'contingency' factors that affect the strength of the relationship between work characteristics and outcomes. In other words, even if team working leads to enriched work design, there are factors that affect whether and how strongly enriched work design leads to enhanced well-being. A simple example is that some individuals do not want greater job autonomy, and therefore these individuals do not necessarily benefit from work enrichment.

Two organisational factors that are likely to affect the relationship between work design characteristics and well-being are described next:

- **Level of uncertainty**

  Research evidence suggests that the greater the degree of uncertainty (i.e., the more complex the situation and the more demands employees need to respond to), the more important it is for effective performance that the team is self-managing. This is because it is in complex situations that rules cannot be anticipated for every situation; nor can supervisors possibly know enough to make all the decisions. Therefore, allowing employees' autonomy to make their own decisions is likely to lead to more timely and more appropriate decision-making.

- **Supportive human resource systems practices**

  If human resource practices do not align with the enriched work design, then work characteristics might not have the positive effects on well-being that are proposed. For example, if employees decision-making responsibilities are expanded, yet they are not given the necessary training or information to make good decisions, then greater autonomy might not lead to the expected positive outcomes such as job satisfaction.

Individuals are also likely to vary in their response to work design characteristics. For example, it has been established that individuals who have a high aspiration for growth and development are more likely to respond to enriched work design. Those responsible for implementing team working need to recognise that employees will vary in how they respond to team working. Allowances should be made for some individuals who do not prefer this mode of working.

What can we conclude from the research?

A key conclusion from this research is that the implementation of team working is not inevitably good for employee well-being, nor is it inevitably bad. The effects of team working on well-being will depend on a number of organisational, design, strategic, individual, and implementation factors, several of which were outlined above and which are further elaborated in the report.

The important point is that organisations need to recognise that they can make choices that have important consequences for employee well-being. By pro-actively considering the factors described above, employers can make choices that enrich employees' work characteristics and thereby promote mental health at work. Employers need to be fully informed about the choices available to them, and the consequences of these choices.

2. ABOUT THE RESEARCH

2.1 BACKGROUND

The issue of poor mental health due to work, or work-related stress, is recognised as an important national issue. There are concerns that levels of occupational stress are high, and increasing among some occupational groups. For example, based on a survey of 8,000 people in the Bristol areas of the UK, the Bristol Stress and Health at Work Study (Smith *et al.,* 2000: HSE, CRR 265/2000) found that about one five workers reported being very or extremely stressed by their work, which is estimated to equate to about five million workers in the UK. The cost to Britain's economy of work-related stress is estimated at 6.7 million working days lost per year, costing society between £3.7 billion and £3.8 billion per year (1995/96 prices, quoted on the HSE website, 1 November 2000). In 1999, the Health and Safety Commission carried out a public consultation exercise on stress. Based on this exercise, and HSE research, the Health and Safety Commission (Press Release C028:00) concluded that:

a) work-related stress is a serious problem
b) work-related stress is a health and safety issue
c) work-related stress can be tackled in part through the application of health and safety legislation

At the same time as this growing recognition of work-related stress and its consequences, vast change is occurring within the modern work place and has the potential to impact on employees' well-being. Global markets, new flexible technologies, and socio-political developments mean organisations are undergoing profound transformations in order to survive and compete. For example:

- there is a growing interest in more flexible forms of working, such as team working
- traditional distinctions between departments are disappearing, a flexible 'boundary less' organisation is reported to be emerging
- there is pressure on organisations to reduce the numbers of staff, to outsource non 'core' businesses, and to create a temporary workforce as a buffer against market fluctuations
- mergers and acquisitions are common place, leading to new organisational forms such as network organisations and lateral organisations

- new information technologies mean that employees no longer need to work in the office – 'virtual' employees can work from home or elsewhere and 'virtual' teams can work together across distances and time zones.

These and other such changes are characteristic of many organisations today.

It is vital that more is learnt about how these various changes in the nature of work affect employee mental health. In recognition of this situation, the Health and Safety Executive (HSE) called for research concerning the psychosocial risks of new ways of working (NWOW, Reference H8). HSE funded research elsewhere has recognised that major organisational change such as team working can, if inappropriately managed, negatively impinge on employee health and safety (HSE, 1996). The research described in this report is a response to the call for research in the psychosocial risks of new ways of working, particularly flexible forms of work organisation, such as team working.

Although team working is a form of work design that has been around for many decades, its use in organisations as a permanent part of the organisational structure is on the increase. Therefore, whilst the concept of team working is not 'new', it does form a new way of working for many organisations.

There are at least two types of implications that team working might have for employee mental health:

a) Team working might be a way of *enhancing employee mental health, or reducing work-related stress.* As described in this report, there is evidence that suggests that, under particular circumstances, team working can promote job satisfaction, reduce stress and enhance employee well-being.

For example, the introduction of autonomous team working (self-managing teams) can enhance employees' job control. Low job control has been identified as a major work-related stressor with negative consequences for employees' mental and physical health (e.g., Stansfield, Head & Marmot, 2000: HSE, CRR 266/2000; Schnall, Landsbergis & Baker, 1994; Karasek & Theorell, 1990). Autonomous team working therefore provides a potential way to reduce the stressor of low job control.

Another HSE-funded study of the effects of 'learning organisations' found that those in learning organisations in which employees are encouraged to continually learn, adapt and meet challenges in creative ways had more positive responses to their work and did their control group (Simpson, 2000: HSE CRR 259/2000). The authors concluded that new working practices can give organisations an opportunity to manage work-related stress in a positive way because established ways of thinking are challenged.

b) On the other hand, there is a danger that flexible work practices such as team working could *damage employees' mental health and escalate stress.* For example, this is likely if inappropriate models of team working are implemented, employees are uninvolved in implementation, or if job control and autonomy is reduced as a result of team working. A reduction in job control brought about by standardisation of procedures is one reason why lean production teams have been criticised and described as 'mean production'.

Given that team working can have either positive or negative implications for well-being, it is important to understand how the positive effects can be enhanced and the negative effects minimised or prevented.

2.2 AIM OF THE RESEARCH

The broad aim of the research was to expand knowledge about the flexible forms of work organisation, particularly team working, affect employees' work-related stress and related well-being outcomes[2] .

Specifically, the research goals were:

a) to conduct and disseminate findings from rigorous investigations of the effects of production team working on employee well-being

b) to prepare the findings in case format to facilitate dissemination to practitioners

c) to outline the existing body of knowledge on team working and mental health, and to integrate the research findings into this body of knowledge.

---

[2] For consistency with the Health and Safety Executive definition (HSE, 1995), we use the term 'work-related stress' to describe negative strain consequences associated with work (also called 'job strain'). The term 'employee well-being' and 'employee mental health' are more general terms, encompassing work-related stress as well as outcomes such as job satisfaction and general psychological health.

2.3 RESEARCH APPROACH AND METHODS

This research reports on three field studies of the implementation of different types of production team working within different companies. The types of teams were as follows:

- flexible work teams (Study 1)
- lean production teams (Study 2)
- self-managed teams (Study 3)

Study 1 and Study 2 build on existing research conducted within two collaborating industrial partners who introduced team working (Parker, Jackson, Sprigg & Whybrow, 1998) and includes a new research site (Study 3). The continuing studies are longitudinal, which enables an understanding of the complex processes involved in organisational interventions and allows for a better understanding of causality.

As far as possible, the studies used multiple methodologies, including the collection and analysis of qualitative (or verbal) data (e.g., interviews) and quantitative (or numerical) data (e.g., surveys) as well as both self-report data and objective data. The information collected is also at the organisational *and* individual level, recording the effect of team working on organisational effectiveness indicators (e.g., absence, safety, on-time deliveries, quality) as well as individual outcomes (e.g., stress, job satisfaction).

Much research on initiatives such as team working draws only on management perceptions, which provides a very narrow and often biased perspective. The current studies consider the effects of team working from the employees' perspectives, as well as from the organisation's perspective.

The importance of conducting systematic and methodologically sound investigations into the effects of team working is highlighted in an HSE-funded review by Kathy Parkes and Timothy Sparkes. These researchers reported that, at the time, there were few methodologically rigorous evaluations of the effect of organisational interventions on work related stress (Parkes & Sparkes, 1998: HSE CRR 193/1998).

3. BACKGROUND: ABOUT TEAM WORKING

Before beginning the discussion about team working, we describe in this section how team working is one of several forms of flexibility that have been identified as occurring within organisations.

3.1 FLEXIBILITY WITHIN TODAY'S ORGANISATIONS

Organisations increasingly need to be agile. They need to be able to respond quickly to changing market demands, to provide customised products and services, and to do so without sacrificing quality. Organisations are no longer the static entities of the past, and flexibility has been identified as key to success in today's fast changing business world.

Four broad types of flexibility have been identified (*see* Box 1)[3], which we briefly describe (*see* Parker & Whybrow, 1998, for a more detailed description).

Box 1: Summary of major types of flexibility

- Flexible forms of work organisation (e.g., team working, multiskilling)
- Flexible techniques and technologies (e.g., just-in-time)
- Financial flexibility (e.g., the creation of a contingent workforce)
- Geographical flexibility (e.g., virtual offices, teleworking, telecommuting)

3.1.1 Flexible forms of work organisation such as team working

The first broad form of flexibility, which is the focus of this research, concerns the way that work is organised and managed. Initiatives such as multiskilling, empowerment, and team working all aim to increase flexibility by restructuring how work is designed. For example, multiskilled employees with a broader knowledge and skill base can carry out multiple tasks and can move to different areas depending on need. Similarly, empowered employees can respond more effectively and efficiently to problems that arise, without needing to defer to others in higher level or specialist positions. Traditionally, these decisions would have been up to supervisors, managers or experts, who were the only people who had the necessary information to make the best decisions. These days, there is an argument for shortening the

[3] It is important to note that our aim is to describe common types of flexibility, but this does not necessarily mean we endorse them as the best management approach.

hierarchy of decision making so that front-line employees can quickly respond to requests or difficulties, which in turn increases the ability of organisations to respond flexibly.

These elements – multiskilling, empowerment, and team working – often come together in the form of *self-managing teams*. We discuss this type of team working as well as other types further in Section 3.2.

3.1.2 Flexible technologies and flexible management techniques

Various flexible technologies and techniques are being introduced in order to deliver the right quantity of products or services, at the right time, without any detriment to quality or escalation of cost. These flexible technologies often co-occur with team working. Some common flexible technologies and techniques within production settings are as follows:

- **Advanced Manufacturing Technology (AMT):** A family of computer-based technologies that have the usual benefits of automation (e.g., consistent product quality, enhanced output levels) but the added advantage of computer control.
- **Just-in-Time (JIT):** A system for minimising capital tied up in inventory and stores by building and delivering products 'just-in'time' for the customer.
- **Total Quality Management (TQM):** A strategy in which quality is no longer seen as a policing and rectification function, but as an integral part of the production process. For example, there is a strong emphasis on making things 'right first time' with TQM programmes, eliminating the need for inspection.
- **Cellular Manufacture:** The grouping of machines, people, and processes into 'cells' where a particular product or type of product is made. Cellular manufacturing is often a pre-cursor to team working.
- **Business Process Engineering (BPR):** The development of systems build around teams which reflect the processes that the business actually works around rather than the operational functions it uses to execute processes.

3.1.3 Financial flexibility

A third form of flexibility is financial flexibility. It is argued that organisations can respond more flexibly to the market through identifying and resourcing core business interests, and by outsourcing non-core operations. Mergers, downsizing, take-overs, the creation of a contingent work force (e.g., a large number of people on temporary employment contracts) and other such organisational transformations are examples of financial flexibility.

3.1.4 Geographical flexibility

Another form of flexibility is geographical flexibility. Primarily due to the growth of information technology, people can work together even though they are separate in time and space. For example, *'virtual teams'* with members from around the world can use technologies such as video-conferencing and electronic mail to share information and knowledge. People can also work in a *'virtual office'* ; that is, employees can work from home or in satellites close to home (teleworking) via electronic communications. The notion of a 'waking week' rather than a 'working week' refers to the fact that people do not necessarily have to come and work in a designated office space for a designated time.

This discussion highlights that, although team working is one important way of achieving greater organisational flexibility, there are other ways. A summary of the major types of flexibility is shown in Box 1 (*see* p.19). It is also important to note that many of these types of flexibility occur in parallel within the same organisation. Our focus is particularly on team working, a prevalent form of flexibility that we describe in greater detail next.

3.2 TEAM WORKING AS A PREVALENT FORM OF FLEXIBILITY

In the previous section, we identified team working as one popular way of achieving organisational flexibility (and indeed other benefits). Over the last decade there has been an increase in the use of team based working in organisations. This is evidenced by the finding that, in the mid 1990's, 55% of UK manufacturing companies reported using team working (Waterson, Clegg, Bolden, Pepper, Warr & Wall, 1997). Another survey in the early 1990's of 560 organisations in Leicestershire found that 76% had adopted team working amongst employees of non-managerial level (Storey, 1994).

This increase in the use of team working is not just a UK phenomenon. For example, a similar trend has been found in the USA with 54% of leading USA companies being found to use team based working (Osterman, 1994). It is also predicted that this trend will continue in the future, and in fact more so than other initiatives such as JIT and TQM (Waterson, Clegg, Bolden, Pepper, Wall & Wall, 1997). Team working is therefore already popular and in the ascendancy (Cordery, 1996).

The move towards team-based working is primarily due to the fact that organisations assume that team working will be beneficial for them. For example, it has been proposed that, because members of self-managing teams have the authority to respond to problems themselves without needing to wait for the supervisors, problems can be dealt with quicker and hence, time will be saved and the financial cost of the problem will be reduced.

Some of the potential benefits of team working, especially self-managing teams, that have been identified include the following:

- improved productivity
- improved quality
- more innovation
- more effective decision-making
- better customer service
- greater employee satisfaction
- decreased costs
- reduced bureaucracy
- a smaller workforce
- reduced time-to-market for products
- a more motivated workforce

As described later in Section 6, research evidence suggests that the above benefits can potentially arise from team working, although there are several factors that can mitigate such benefits and even result in team working having negative effects for employees and/or organisations.

Prior to looking at how team working affects individuals and organisations, it is important to have a good understanding of what is meant by teams and team effectiveness, and the important ways that teams vary.

3.3 WHAT IS TEAM WORKING?

Teams are more than just groups of employees fulfilling a similar organisation function, or employees located in the same part of the organisation. Mueller *et al.,* (2000, p.1399) recently defined teams as "groups of employees, normally between three and 15 members, who meet with some regularity in order to work interdependently on fulfilling a specific task".

In a similar vein, West, Borrill & Unsworth (1998) suggested three criteria for a group to be considered as a team:

- the group needs to have a defined organisational function and identity
- the group must possess shared objectives or goals
- the team members must have interdependent roles

That is, the members of the team (and others within the organisation) must recognise that groups of people as members of that team, and the team must have a specific task (or set of tasks) to perform. The members of the team must also share a set of goals or objectives. For example, they might be expected, as a team, to produce a certain number of products per week or to provide a service with a particular level of quality and efficiency. Finally, the team members must need to co-ordinate and collaborate with each other (in other words, have interdependent roles) in order to get their job done. Although these defining elements of a team seem rather obvious, organisations often neglect to design teams with these features (e.g., they fail to ensure they have shared goals).

Box 2: Core features of team working

- A group with a defined organisational function and identity
- A group with shared objectives and goals
- Interdependent roles (i.e., team members need to co-operate to get the job done)

3.4 WHAT IS 'EFFECTIVE' TEAM WORKING?

The above definition describes a team, but what is an *effective team?* Four criteria that are recognised as constituting an effective team or group (e.g., Cohen, Ledford & Sprietzer, 1996; Guzzo & Dickson, 1996; Hackman, 1987; Sundstrom *et al.,* 1990) are shown in Box 3. In other words, an effective team is one that promotes organisational benefits as well as individual mental health and job satisfaction. It is also important that the team is sustainable. If the team is successful, but the membership cannot be sustained (e.g., due to irreconcilable personality differences) then it will not be effective in the long term.

Box 3: Key criteria of team effectiveness

- Performance (e.g., high productivity, quality and cost effectiveness)
- Team member well-being (e.g., high job satisfaction, organisational commitment and low stress)
- Team member behaviour (e.g., low absence and turnover)
- Team viability (i.e., a team that can continue to work together)

Whilst the focus of the current research is mostly on employee criteria (particularly the effect of team working on employees; mental health), it is important to also consider organisational and performance outcomes. The principle motive of most companies that introduce team working is to enhance the performance of their organisation, and therefore it is important to investigate the organisational impact of team working.

The four effectiveness criteria can be related. For example, research suggests that employee well-being is related to subsequent performance (Wright *et al.,* 1993) and companies in which employees report high job satisfaction and organisational commitment are found to have higher financial performance over a ten year period (West & Patterson, 1998). Research also suggests that stressed individuals are more likely to be absent (e.g., Ulleberg & Rundmo, 1997) and less likely to continue working at the company (e.g., Cavanaugh, Boswell, Roehling & Bourdreau, 2000).

More specific criteria for effective team working can also be identified, depending in part on the strategic goals of the organisation. For example, in some cases, it is hoped that team working will not simply result in teams being more efficient, but that team working will enhance employees' innovation and use of personal initiative.

3.5 TYPES OF TEAM WORKING

There are many different forms of team working being used within organisations, and it is important to distinguish between them. Appelbaum & Batt (1994) pointed out that researchers often fail to distinguish between different forms of team working, which is partly why research findings about their effects are often inconsistent. Indeed, Cannon-Bowers, Osler & Flanagan (1992) list a total of 20 different types of teams, including problem solving teams, quality circles, semi-autonomous teams, multi-disciplinary teams and product development groups. Mueller *et al.,* (2000, p.1399) identified a range of ways that teams differ from each other, such as whether the teams are temporary or permanent structures, where people in the teams are from, and whether team members are voluntary or not.

Next, we describe in more detail the three key dimensions that differentiate the types of teams we focus on in our research from other teams.

3.5.1 Aspects that differentiate our teams from other teams

- **Information or production/service teams**

  One key criteria distinguishing between the different types of teams is whether they *process information* (e.g., planning, creating and deciding) or whether they *produce goods or services* (Devine, Clayton, Philips, Dunford & Melner, 1990). In this report we focus on those teams that produce goods or services.

- **Temporary or permanent team structures**

  Teams that produce goods and services are typically quite permanent team structures, involving team members who are grouped together in order to carry out their core work tasks in an on-going way. In contrast, teams that process information (e.g., software development teams) are often created on a temporary basis to solve a particular problem and then disband. In this report we focus on relatively permanent teams.

- **Focus on core tasks**

  Another dimension is the extent to which the *team activities involve core tasks.* Sometimes, the team activities are carried out off the job (such as in continuous improvement teams), whereas in other teams the team activities are a core part of the job (e.g., teams focused on building products or delivering services). Here, we focus on relatively permanent teams where individuals are grouped in order to carry out their core work tasks.

Box 4: Defining aspects of teams focused on in this research

- Teams that produce goods (mostly production teams) rather than teams that process information
- Permanent team structures as opposed to temporary team structures set up to solve particular problems
- Teams that focus on core work tasks

3.5.2 Aspects that differentiate our teams from each other

Although we are focusing on relatively permanent teams that carry out core work tasks to produce goods and services, these teams still vary in quite fundamental ways, as described below.

- **Degree of autonomy and involvement in decision-making**

  One of the most important dimensions that distinguishes between types of teams concerns the *amount of autonomy* that teams have in carrying out their tasks. Banker *et al.,* (1996) developed a Team Autonomy Continuum where at one extreme is the traditional work group in which a supervisor continues to manage the team in the traditional way by controlling and directing the day-to-day work activities of the team. At the other extreme is the self-managing team in which the team members are themselves responsible for the day-to-day running of the team (e.g., team members decide who does what, when and how).

Another useful categorisation is the Teamwork Matrix developed by Marchington (2000). In this matrix two dimensions define a profile of autonomy and involvement. The first dimension is the *'degree of involvement'* that the teams have, which refers to the degree of autonomy or discretion that the teams have over decision-making. This dimension is very similar to Banker *et al's.,* (1996) Team Autonomy Continuum.

- **Scope of involvement**

  The second dimension in Marchington's matrix is the *'scope of involvement'* that teams have. This refers to the type of decisions that teams are involved in and is based on a distinction outlined by Gospel & Palmer (1993). Gospel & Palmer argued that the degree of autonomy that teams have can involve three types of activities:

  - the organisation of work (e.g., methods of working and the allocation of work)
  - employee relations (e.g., recruitment of team members, disciplining team members)
  - management-employee relations (e.g., acting as representatives of the team, negotiating rewards and budgets for the team)

- **Type of team leadership**

  Strongly related to the dimensions of 'degree of autonomy' and 'scope of involvement' is the model of team leadership. The type of leadership typically co-varies with the degree of team autonomy and scope of involvement.

  Thus, a *traditional work group model* is one in which a supervisor external to the team controls and directs the team, such as by allocating tasks and making key decisions. Employee autonomy and scope of involvement is low.

  A *team-leader* model is one in which there is a designated hands-on team leader. These teams vary in the degree to which employees have autonomy and involvement, depending on the style of the team leader (e.g., participative vs. authoritative) and structural characteristics. A team-leader led team can be relatively self-managing, depending on the style and role of the team leader.

A *fully self-managing team* is one in which team members are themselves responsible for the day-to-day running of the team (e.g., team members decided who does what, when and how).

- **Degree of multiskilling or specialisation**

  A similar categorisation to those above is what Cordery (1996) referred to as the *degree of intra-group task specialisation,* or multiskilling (Cordery, 1996).

  - vertical multiskilling refers to team members learning elements of the supervisory role
  - horizontal multiskilling refers to learning tasks from traditionally separate occupational or job families, such as a mine operator learning to drive a truck and carry out laboratory tasks
  - depth multiskilling refers to developing skills within the same occupational or skill group but which usually have a different job title, such as a mechanical tradesperson learning advanced hydraulics.

  Cordery (1996) suggested that self-managing teams tend to be characterised by medium to high degrees of vertical multiskilling and horizontal multiskilling but low levels of depth multiskilling. Groups can also vary in the *extent to which members control all of the relevant support tasks,* such as quality and maintenance. Some teams control all of these aspects, whereas other teams contain very few support elements.

- **Degree of standardisation of procedures within teams**

  Teams vary in the extent to which their core tasks are standardised. Recent years have seen the growth of 'lean production teams', which have a heavy emphasis on the development of, and adherence to, standard operating procedures. We describe lean production teams further in the next section.

Box 5: Characteristics that differ across the teams we investigated in this research

- Degree of autonomy/involvement of team members
- Scope of involvement of team members
- The model of team leadership
- Degree of multiskilling or specialisation of team members
- Degree of standardisation of procedures within teams

In the summary, it is clear that there are important variations in types of teams. These differences need to be considered when evaluating the effects of team working. For example, research shows large differences in impact depending on whether the team is self-managing or a traditional work group. Part of the goal of research into team working is therefore to identify the salient dimensions that differentiate teamwork and to determine what types of teams are best for which circumstances. The most important distinctions are usually the degree and scope of team involvement in decision-making. However, it is also important to consider the presence or absence of standard operating procedures and the nature and structure of team leadership.

3.5.3 Types of team focused on in this research

In this research, we focused on four types of prevalent teams that arise from combinations of the above characteristics:

- traditional work groups
- lean production teams
- self-managing teams
- flexible work teams

These types of team vary in their position in Marchington's Team Work Matrix with traditional work groups having the lowest degree of scope of employee involvement, followed by lean production teams, flexible work teams, and then self-managing teams having the greatest scope and degree of involvement. We summarise the key characteristics of these teams below:

- **Traditional work groups**

  Traditional work groups are controlled and managed by a first line supervisor in their performance of core production tasks. These teams have no involvement in support activities and little or no input into the day to day running of their work area (Banker *et al.*, 1996). That is, traditional work teams have both a low degree of involvement and a low scope of involvement. They are also often not 'teams' in the sense that they have low task interdependence and do not possess shared work goals. Most production organisations have some form of traditional work groups prior to implementing team working.

- **Lean production teams**

  Lean production is a method of production that focuses on removing 'waste' or non-value added activities from the production process in order to deliver precisely the right quality and quantity of raw materials, parts or complete products when they are needed to the next stage of the production process (Monden, 1994). There is a heavy emphasis on removing buffers between work stages so that work can flow smoothly (as seen in 'just-in-time' methods of production), as well as a heavy emphasis on process simplification and standardisation.

Lean production teams, therefore, are groups of employees who work very closely together to do whatever is necessary to keep production going. The teams are characterised by the standard operating procedures that regulate team members' work. Typically there is a first line supervisor who manages the team, and often there are off-line continuous improvement activities in which the team members work on simplifying and standardising procedures (Benders & Hootegem, 2000). Thus, the work of lean production teams is heavily production-focused with little employee involvement in management or support activities (Banker *et al*, 1996; Delbridge, Lowe & Oliver, 2000). As such, lean production teams also typically have a low degree of involvement and a low scope of involvement relative to self-managing teams or flexible work groups. However, the use of off-line continuous improvement activities does increase the scope of involvement that lean production teams have relative to traditional work groups. On the other hand, the use of standard operating procedures means that lean production teams typically have less autonomy regarding how they go about conducting their production tasks than traditional work groups.

- **Self-managed teams**

  Self-managed teams are characterised by having a high degree of involvement and autonomy. These are the rarest kind of team. The main characteristics of these teams are that they have responsibility for the performance of the team (e.g., Manz & Sims, 1993; Cohen & Ledford, 1994), and the autonomy to make decisions regarding issues such as the methods of working, assigning members to tasks, solving production and interpersonal problems, and conducting meetings (e.g., Cummings, 1978; Wellins, Byham & Wilson, 1991). In fact, Wall, Kemp, Jackson & Clegg (1996) argue that the key feature of self-managing teams is a high degree of self-determination in the management of day-to-day tasks. External supervisors rather than 'managing the team', as the case in lean production and traditional teams, instead act as facilitators of the team (e.g., training and coaching the teams) (Manz & Sims, 1993).

Within the literature, various types of self-managing teams have been described. For example, autonomous work groups (Cummings, 1978; Clement, 1996), semi-autonomous work groups, high performance work teams (Banker *et al.*, 1996), self-regulating teams (Pearce & Ravlin, 1987), self-directed teams (Murakami, 1997) and self-designed teams (Banker *et al.*, 1996). Often there is little distinction, either within the research literature or in practice, between these types of self-managing teams (Charles, 2000). However, although all of these types of self-managing team are characterised by a high degree of autonomy they do tend to vary in terms of the scope of involvement that they are given. For example, autonomous work teams and self-managing teams tend to merely have autonomy over the organisation of day to day work, whereas self-directing teams tend to also have autonomy over employee relations and self-designing teams tend to also have involvement in manager-employee relations.

The leadership of self-managing teams varies. In 'true' self-managing teams, there is an external facilitator of the team (this person usually manages several teams), but the team itself is self-lead. Another mode is to have a team leader, with the team leader acting purely as a point of reference for external personnel and the team members largely self-managing. The team leader position is often rotated amongst the team members and the choice of the team leader is made by the team members. Some organisations introduce team leaders at the start of team working, with the intention of phasing out team leaders when the team becomes more self-managing. A danger with this approach is that team leaders simply take on a supervisory role and the team does not become self-managing.

- **Flexible work teams**

  Flexible work teams are those in which the team members are multiskilled and able to help each other carry out their tasks. It is expected that they will provide benefits in terms of efficiency and flexibility (e.g., team members can cover for others if they are absent). Flexible work teams have a greater degree and scope of involvement than traditional work groups, but they do not have as much involvement or autonomy as self-managing teams. They are usually led by a 'hands on' team leader, or a team member that works within the team but also has a role in the running of the team. Although the role of the team leader can vary dramatically, affecting the level of team member autonomy and involvement, the team leader is usually expected to adopt more of a coaching orientation than is the case in traditional work groups. Typically, the team has a shared set of goals, and tasks are interdependent. Flexible work groups are often considered a 'safer' option because managers can often fear a loss of control with self-managing teams.

Box 6: Team types focused on in this research

- Traditional work groups
- Lean production teams
- Self-managing teams
- Flexible work teams

4. THEORETICAL PERSPECTIVES ON TEAM WORKING

There are three established theoretical approaches that inform team-working developments. These are briefly described for those who are interested in theory of team working.

4.1 SOCIO-TECHNICAL SYSTEMS THEORY

The Socio-Technical Systems (STS) approach originated in the 1950's at the Tavistock Institute of Human Relations based in London (Emery & Trist, 1960; Rice, 1958; Trist & Bamforth, 1951). The basic premise of STS is that there are two sub-systems within organisations, the technical and the social sub-systems (Pasmore, 1988; Cummings & Strivastva, 1977; Emery, 1959). These are as follows:

- technical aspects – such as the tools, techniques, strategies, skills and knowledge that are need to accomplish the tasks
- social aspects – such as the relationship between employees and technology, and the relationships between employees

STS theory advocates that the work system should balance *both the technical and social aspects of work* (Cummings, 1978; Emery & Trist, 1969; Susman, 1976). Maximising both the social and technical aspects of work is called *joint optimisation* (Cummings & Molloy, 1977). Focusing on only one sub-system will not lead to effectiveness. For example, a company that solely focuses on having the best tools, techniques, strategies, skills and knowledge for the job, yet ignores how the employees are effected by the system or how employees relate to one another, will be ineffective. Instead an organisation must strive to enhance both the technological and the social aspects of work. Some key principles of the STS approach are shown in Box 7.

Box 7: Key socio-technical systems principles

- design processes should be compatible with desired design outcomes (e.g., participative design for participative systems)
- methods of working should be minimally specified
- variances in the work processes (e.g., breakdowns, changes in product requirements) should be handled at the source
- those who need resources should have access to and authority over them
- team member roles should be multifunctional and multiskilled
- redesign should be continuous, not a 'once and for all' change

Self-managing teams have been suggested as a tool that enables the joint optimisation of the technical and social sub-systems (e.g., Cummings, 1978). By providing an enriched and motivating work environment, self-managing teams satisfy the social needs of employees whilst creating a team in which the technical aspects of the teams' tasks can best be addressed (e.g., faster problem-solving and decision-making due to the teams not having to defer decisions to their supervisors).

In contrast, the STS approach is less compatible with the idea of lean production since the standard operating procedures are likely to hinder the social needs of employees.

4.2 THE JOB CHARACTERISTICS MODEL

One of the most influential models of work design is the Job Characteristics Model (JCM) developed by Hackman & Oldham (1975, 1976). The JCM identifies five job characteristics that are proposed to lead to employee motivation, satisfaction and effectiveness (*see* Box 8).

Box 8: Core job characteristics that are proposed to enhance motivation and performance

- Skill variety (a varied range of tasks)
- Task identity (doing a whole piece of work rather than a fragment)
- Task significance (doing meaningful work)
- Autonomy (discretion to make decisions)
- Feedback from the job

The JCM asserts that these job characteristics result in greater employee satisfaction, motivation and performance as well as reduced absenteeism and turnover. In addition, the effects predicted by this model are argued to be greater for those individuals who value challenge and personal development (i.e., those with high growth need strength).

When applied at the team level, the JCM overlaps a great deal with the recommendations that arise out of socio-technical systems theory. For example, members of self-managing teams should have variety, work together on a whole product or service, act autonomously, and receive feedback on their work. Indeed, it is for this reason that Hackman (1987) extended the JCM to apply at the group level (*see Section 4.3*) and even argued that autonomous work groups have the potential to be more powerful than individual forms of job design because they can encompass larger and more complete pieces of work (Hackman, 1977).

4.3 INPUT – PROCESS - OUTPUT APPROACH TO TEAM EFFECTIVENESS

A third approach to understanding team working is an input – process – output model. Many models of team effectiveness that have been developed take an 'input – process – output' approach to team effectiveness (e.g., Campion, Medsker & Higgs, 1993; Cohen, Ledford & Spreitzer, 1996; Gladstein, 1984; Hackman, 1987).

- *Inputs* are considered to include knowledge, skills and abilities of group members, the composition of the team, and aspects of organisational context such as the tasks and associated objectives, reward systems, information systems and training resources
- *Process* refers to the interactions among group members, for example information exchange, patterns of participation in decision making and social support
- *Outputs* include the group performance, but may also include group viability and team member well-being, growth and satisfaction

The most basic variation of this approach is that team inputs influence team processes, which in turn influence team outputs (*see Figure 1a*). However, Hackman (1987) has also suggested that there may be a direct link between inputs and outputs (*see Figure 1b*) or there maybe both direct and indirect links between inputs and outcomes (*see Figure 1c*).

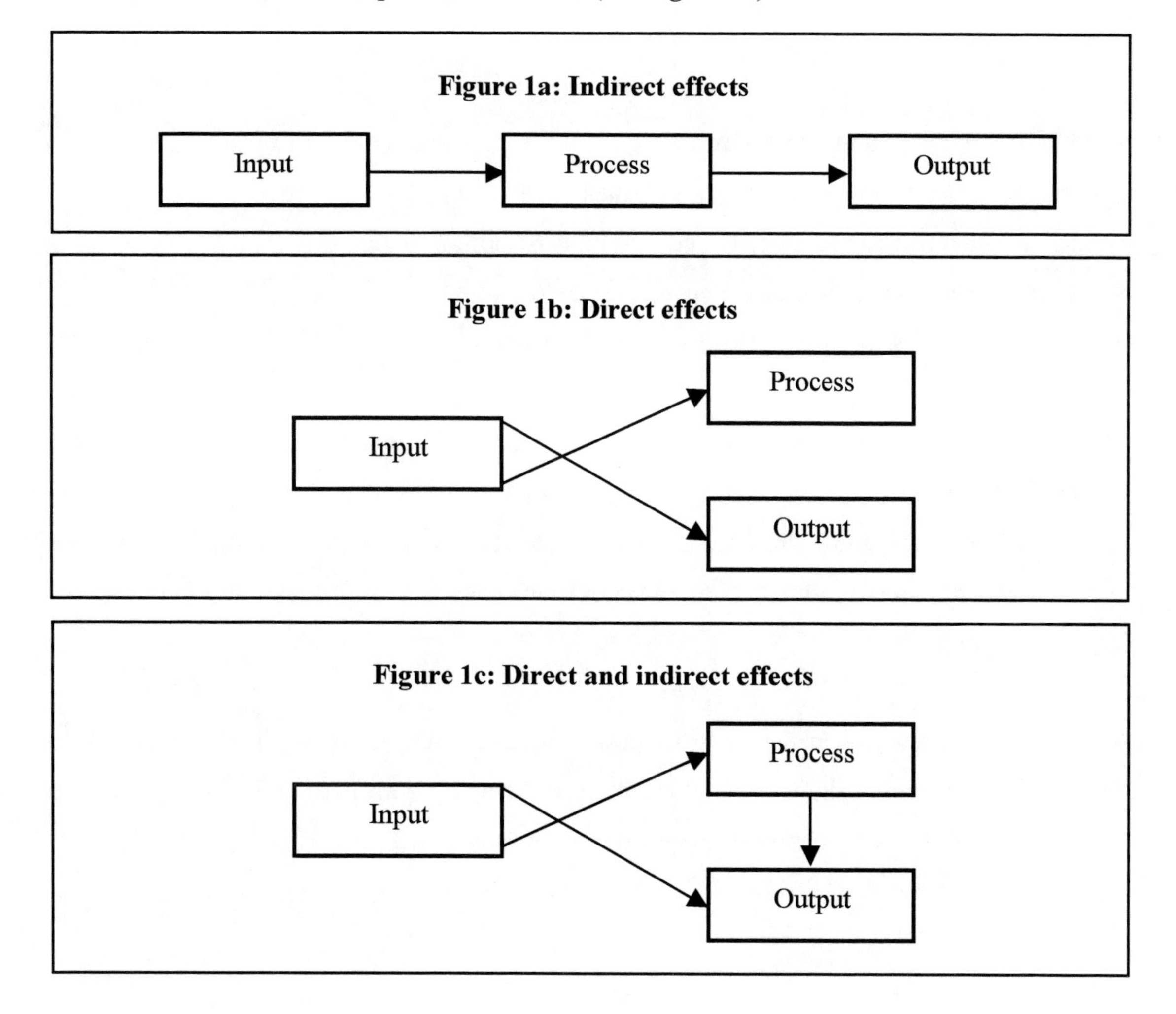

Hackman (1987) developed one of the most influential models of team working. It is suggested that increases in various process criteria (i.e., effort, knowledge and appropriateness of task performance strategies), given the presence of the necessary material resources, will lead to greater team effectiveness.

Three levers to enhance the process criteria, or the inputs to the model, are as follows:

- group design, which is partly about structuring tasks so that people have variety, autonomy and so on, but additionally involves making appropriate decisions about the composition of the group (the right number of people, the right mix of individuals, etc.) and ensuring the group has appropriate norms about performance.
- organisational context, which concerns having the appropriate reward, education and information systems to support and reinforce task performance.
- group synergy, which is concerned with features that help the group to interact, such as reducing process losses.

Another influential model of team effectiveness was developed by Campion and colleagues (Campion *et al.,* 1993; Campion *et al.,* 1996). In this model, five inputs are suggested to contribute to team effectiveness:

- job design (task variety, task significance, task identity, autonomy and feedback)
- interdependence (in terms of tasks, goals and objectives)
- composition (e.g., size, diversity and flexibility of skills)
- context (e.g., training and management support)
- processes (e.g., social support and workload stress)

However, research does suggest that these factors vary in their relative importance (*see Section 6.2.1*). Campion *et al's* model is very similar to that of Hackman, however, it is more comprehensive since group design is separated into three categories allowing the distinction between the job design, the degree of interdependence amongst team members and the composition of the team.

These models are useful in that they suggest a broader range of factors that influence team working effectiveness, although one criticism (Parker & Wall, 1998) is that the precise mediating and moderating pathways have rarely been fully tested.

Box 9: Aspects that are likely to characterise effective teams

Based on the above theories, teams are likely to be most effective when:

- Members have tasks with variety and significance
- Members have autonomy over decision making so that they can control problems as and when they occur
- Members receive clear feedback on their performance
- There is interdependence between team members' tasks (i.e. the tasks are designed such that team members need to co-operate with each other)
- Teams are cohesive, and there is trust and good communication
- There is effective leadership for the team
- There are appropriate organisational supports for team working (e.g., training and resources)
- Teams are of an appropriate size and composition

5. EFFECTS OF TEAM WORKING ON ORGANISATATIONS AND INDIVIDUALS

In this section, we outline research findings from the academic literature concerning the effects of implementing team working on organisations and individuals.

5.1 TEAM-BASED WORKING

In terms of the effect of team working on employee well-being, comparative evidence suggests that employees who work in teams have better well-being and motivation than employees who work alone (e.g., Moch, 1980; Greller, Parson & Mitchell, 1992; Berggren, 1991; Carter & West, 1999). However, such evidence is purely comparative and thus cannot be completely relied upon.

For example, it could be that people who are drawn to jobs where they work alone are fundamentally different from those individuals who are drawn to jobs that involve working with others. However, longitudinal studies have also found that the implementation of team working can increase job satisfaction (Wall & Clegg, 1981; Cordery, Mueller & Smith, 1991; Pearson, 1992) and organisational commitment (Cordery, Mueller & Smith, 1991) beyond that of individual based working.

Research has also shown that team working can lead to better performance and productivity (Levine & D'Andrea-Tyson, 1990; Cotton, 1993; Applebaum & Batt, 1994; Weldon & Weingart, 1994; Pasmore, 1978). In fact, Macy & Izumi (1993) found that the interventions that brought about the largest effects upon the financial performance of organisations were team development initiatives and the creation of autonomous work groups.

However, the majority of studies have been cross-sectional studies comparing areas where team working is operating with those where individual based working was used. As such the majority of research does not adequately test the effect of implementing team working. Rather studies should be longitudinal investigations that assess employees before and after team working has been implemented. Unfortunately, too few studies of this nature have been conducted, thus the conclusions that can be made are limited. In addition, those studies that have used a rigorous research design have tended to find inconclusive results regarding the effect of the implementation of team working. For example, although Wall & Clegg (1981) found that performance was better after the implementation of autonomous work groups, Cordery, Mueller & Smith (1991) found that turnover and absenteeism were greater in autonomous work groups.

In general therefore, research evidence suggests that team working is beneficial to employee well-being and can (at least sometimes) be beneficial for performance.

5.2 SELF-MANAGED TEAMS

Other research has specifically investigated the effectiveness of self-managed team working. Theoretically, self-managed teams (SMTs) should be particularly beneficial since by definition they have high autonomy that has been found to be positively associated with both performance (e.g., Campion *et al.,* 1993, 1996; Cohen *et al.,* 1996) and well-being (e.g., Campion *et al.,* 1993, 1996; Cordery *et al.,* 1991).

In terms of employee well-being, we again find evidence of the benefits of self-managed team working (e.g., Jackson, Sprigg & Parker, 2000; Spector & O'Connell, 1994; Kirkman & Rosen, 1996). Plus, as with team working, generally these findings appear to hold under the scrutiny of rigorous longitudinal research designs (e.g., Wall *et al.,* 1986; Cohen & Ledford, 1994).

In terms of performance, many studies report evidence of benefits of SMTs (e.g., Cohen & Ledford, 1994; Elmuti & Kathawala, 1999; Banker *et al.,* 1966). For example, SMTs have also been found to be associated with improvements in problem-management actions and strategies (Tesluk & Mathieu, 1999), increased quality (Hansen & Rasmussen, 1995), increased levels of innovation (Walton, 1977), decreased absenteeism (Walton 1977; Hansen & Rasmussen, 1995), decreased turnover (Walton, 1977) and reduced accident rates (Goodman, 1979; Walton, 1977). In some cases, the productivity gains are suggested to be due to the reduced costs that are associated with the removal of supervisors rather than greater efficiency (Wall *et al.,* 1986).

Despite such evidence, in a review of the literature, Goodman *et al* (1988) concluded that autonomous work teams had only a modest impact on productivity and that there were no clear trends with regard to absenteeism and turnover. In addition, as with the evidence for team working generally, the majority of such studies are cross-sectional comparisons. More rigorous studies of the implementation of self-managing teams have been rather mixed in their conclusions, with some studies not finding particularly strong performance effects (e.g. Wall *et al.,* 1986), whereas others have had very promising results (e.g. Batt, 1999). Clearly more research is needed to fully understand the productivity benefits of self-managing teams, and to identify factors that might enhance or inhibit whether self-managing teams yield performance gains.

5.3 LEAN PRODUCTION TEAMS

Very little research has investigated lean production teams and those studies that have been conducted have tended to find contradictory evidence. For example, two studies conducted by Jackson and colleagues found very different effects of the introduction of just-in-time (which is a key element of lean production) on employee well-being. Whilst the introduction of just-in-time decreased job satisfaction in one study (Jackson & Martin, 1996), it was found to increase job satisfaction in another study (Mullarkey, Jackson & Parker, 1995). The latter finding was primarily attributed to the participative style in which just-in-time was introduced, which allowed employees to preserve their already reasonably high levels of autonomy. More recently, Jackson & Mullarkey (2000) found there were little overall differences in work-related stress for those in lean production teams compared to those in traditional methods of working. They attributed this finding to the fact that the lean production teams improved some aspects of work (higher use of skills and greater social contact) but had detrimental effects on other aspects of work (e.g. lower individual timing control).

This inconsistency in findings parallels the debate within the literature. Many researchers have highlighted the potential negative effects of lean production teams (sometimes referred to as 'mean production' teams) on employees. For example, Turnbull (1988) suggested that the removal of buffer stocks between work units that occurs with lean production means employees are less able to leave the work station, thus "recreating the rhythm of assembly-line pacing in plants where there were previously opportunities for workers to determine (to some extent) their own work pace" (p.13).

On the other hand, Womack, Jones & Roos (1990, pp.13-14, 99-102), in their classic text on lean production in auto manufacturing, argued that, by rotating jobs and sharing responsibilities, multiskilled workers in the best Japanese companies have enriched jobs. "The freedom to control one's work replaces the mind numbing stress of mass production. Armed with the skills they need to control their environment, workers in a lean plant have the opportunity to think actively (indeed proactively) to solve workplace problems. This creative tension makes work humanly fulfilling".

Recently, aiming to resolve these conflicting views, Landsbergis *et al.*, (1998) reviewed surveys and case studies investigating lean production, particularly within auto manufacturing companies. They found little evidence that workers are 'empowered' under lean production systems. Indeed, the evidence was that lean production intensifies work demands and work pace, with increases in decision-making authority and skill levels being very modest and/or temporary. Some evidence suggested that, in jobs with physical ergonomic stressors (such as manufacturing jobs), lean production appears to lead to increased rates of musculoskeletal disorders. Nevertheless, Landsbergis *et al.*, (1998) acknowledged that their conclusions are limited by the lack of well-designed studies on the topic, and they advocated more systematic investigation of the effects of new production systems on employees' work design and mental health outcomes.

5.4 CONCLUSION

The implementation of team working can be beneficial to effectiveness, especially in terms of enhancing employee well-being and job satisfaction. However, the beneficial effects are not as great or as consistent as we would expect from the theory, particular when it comes to enhancing organisational performance. There is also little evidence for positive effects of lean production teams, and indeed there is quite a lot of evidence that lean production has negative effects on employees' mental and physical health. In the next section, we synthesise existing research, and incorporate findings from our own research, to propose a model that will enhance understanding of why, when and how teams working has a positive impact on effectiveness. We focus primarily on the link between team working and employee well-being, although many of the same suggestions are likely to apply to performance outcomes.

6. PROPOSED MODEL OF TEAM WORKING AND ITS EFFECT ON WELL -BEING

Based on an analysis of the literature, and the research described in Section 8, the following is proposed as a conceptual framework for understanding the effect of implementing team working (*see Figure 2*). This framework draws on a model of work design developed in previous research (Parker, Jackson, Sprigg & Whybrow, 1998).

Figure 2. Model of team working effectiveness
(based on the work design model proposed by Parker, Jackson, Sprigg & Whybrow, 1998)

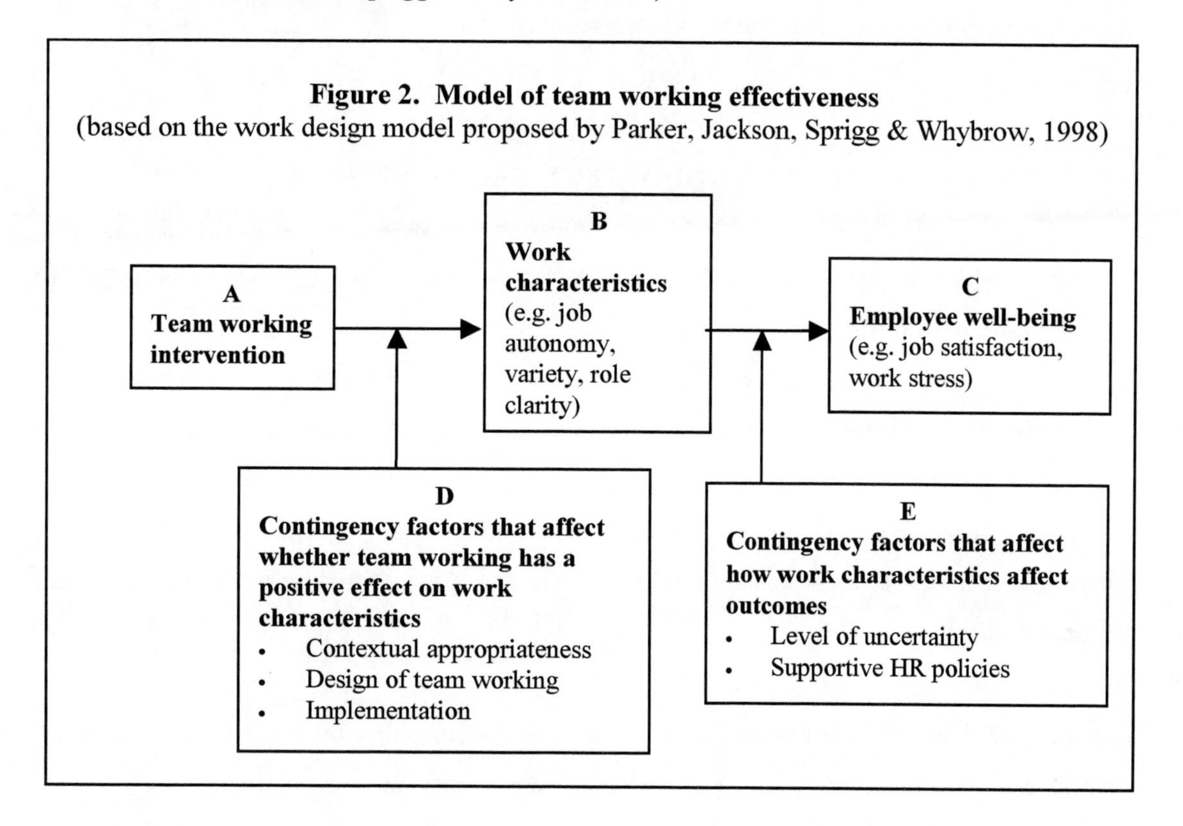

The framework proposes that work design characteristics such as job autonomy (B) affect employee well-being (C). Therefore, it is proposed that the effect of team working (A) on employee well-being (C) depends, at least in part, on how team working (A) impacts on work design characteristics (B).

The model further proposes that there are conditions (or 'contingency factors', D) that affect how team working (A) and work characteristics (B) are linked, as well as other contingency factors (E) that affect how work characteristics (B) and well-being outcomes (C) are linked. For example, it is suggested that the strategy for team working, contextual factors, and implementation factors all influence and shape the effect of team working on work design characteristics.

The more general version of this model developed by Parker *et al.,* (1998) also proposes more specific processes, or mechanisms, that underpin the link between work design (B) and outcomes such as well-being (C). For example, increased autonomy is likely to give employees the opportunity to do a broader range of tasks, and undertaking these tasks will give employees a greater sense of confidence in their ability to do tasks (Parker, 1998). In turn, these feelings of self-confidence might promote better well-being. Such potential mechanisms have not been explored in the in this research, therefore, they are not elaborated here.

Each of the key elements of the model are described further.

6.1 WORK CHARACTERISTICS (B) AFFECT EMPLOYEE WELL-BEING (C)

6.1.1 Proposition 1: Enriched work design that does not involve excessive demands will enhance employee well-being.

The above proposition is based on a large body of research concerning the link between work characteristics and well-being. Within the research literature, there is an abundance of research that, on the whole, supports a link between work characteristics such as job autonomy and outcomes such as job satisfaction and employee motivation (Parker & Wall, 1998; Griffin *et al.*, 1981; Fred & Ferris, 1987; Koelman, 1985). There is also evidence that work characteristics can affect mental and physical health.

For example, a lack of job control has been identified as resulting in stress-related outcomes, such as poor mental health in men and alcohol dependence in women (Stansfield, Head & Marmot, 200: HSE, CRR 266/2000). Other evidence (e.g., Schnall, Landsbergis & Baker, 1994; Landsbergis *et al.,* 1994; Karasek & Theorell, 1990; Johnson, Hall & Theorell, 1989; Kristensen, 1996) suggests that jobs with high demands and low decision latitude (low control and skill variety) are a risk factor for hypertension and cardiovascular disease (CVD). For example, in the Cornell Worksite Blood Pressure study, working men repeatedly exposed to job strain over three years have systolic blood pressures that are at least 10mm Hg greater than men not repeatedly exposed to job strain (Schnall *et al.,* 1998).

Some important work design characteristics for employee well-being that have been identified (e.g., Hackman & Oldham, 1980; Karasek & Theorell, 1990; Parker & Wall, 1998) are described in Box 10. Essentially, high levels of these characteristics make an 'enriched job'.

Box 10: Important work characteristics for promoting well-being

- Job autonomy/decision-making authority
- A lack of job pacing
- Skill variety and opportunity to develop new skills
- Feedback about performance
- Carrying out a whole task and a meaningful job
- Reasonable levels of work load demands
- Clear goals (role clarity)
- Consistency in what is expected (absence of role conflict)
- Positive relationships with colleagues

As we describe later (*see Section 6.4*), however, there are some contingency factors (E) that are likely to mitigate the relationship between work characteristics (B) and well-being (C).

6.2 TEAM WORKING (A) AND EMPLOYEE WELL-BEING (C): MEDIATING ROLE OF WORK CHARACTERISTICS (B)

6.2.1 Proposition 2: The effect of team working on employee well-being will depend on how team working affects work design characteristics.

The model proposes that the effect on team working (A) on outcomes such as employee job stress and job satisfaction (C) depends, at least in part, on how team working affects work characteristics (B).

As described above, there are well-established links between work design (B) and employee well-being (C). Thus, it is reasonable to expect that if team working (A) has a positive effect on work design characteristics (B), then positive outcomes of team working are expected. For example, if team working enhances work characteristics such as job control and task variety, and does not have any other negative effects, then team working should lead to greater job satisfaction and lower work-related stress. Likewise, if team working increases stressful aspects of work, such as role conflict, role overload or role ambiguity, without out compensatory positive consequences for jobs, it will be associated with more stress. In some cases, team working might have positive consequences for some work design characteristics and negative consequences for other work design characteristics, therefore resulting in no overall impact on well-being.

Support for this proposition that the effect of team working depends on how it impacts on work design comes from studies investigating team effectiveness. A cross-sectional study by Campion, Papper & Medsker (1996) showed strongest predictors of team effectiveness (both in terms of performance and employee well-being) were process characteristics (such as the degree of social support and communication within the team) as well as work design characteristics (the degree of self-management, variety, etc.). These findings largely replicated an earlier test of the same framework (Campion, Medsker & Higgs, 1993). A recent meta-analysis by Stewart (2000) found that, in terms of employee well-being, task characteristics such as job autonomy were found to have the strongest relationship (team processes were also important). Team working studies therefore point to the importance of work design as a determinant of outcomes such as employee well-being.

Some studies of lean production teams also demonstrate this proposition. Jackson & Mullarkey (2000) found that although lean production teams had no overall effect on employees' stress or job satisfaction, this was because the positive effects on work design (e.g., increased task variety) were counteracted by negative effects on work design (e.g., decreased autonomy). They concluded that lean production teams could have negative and positive consequences for employees, with the net effect depending on exactly how the lean production teams have affected the work design.

Our research in this project clearly shows that where team working has had a positive effect on work design (e.g., resulting in enhanced team member autonomy), then there were benefits for team well-being.

For example, Study 2 describes a situation in which lean teams were introduced within some areas of production. The teams involved groups working together to standardise their work procedures, and therefore represent an early form of lean production teams. In this study, there was evidence that being in participative and supported teams acted to buffer employees somewhat from the negative effects of broader site wide changes. However, if teams were introduced in a way that did not allow for employee participation, and if the team activities were not supported by others then the lean teams had negative effects for employee well-being. These findings support the argument that the effect of team working on employee well-being will depend on how team working affects work characteristics. The only teams where there was some positive mental health benefit were those where team activities were supported and where team members had influence over decision-making.

6.3 CONDITIONS UNDER WHICH TEAM WORKING HAS A POSITIVE EFFECT ON WORK CHARACTERISTICS

6.3.1 Proposition 3: The effect of team working (A) on work characteristics (B) depends on the design of team working, as well as implementation and contextual factors (D).

We propose that the relationship between team working and work design is a contingent one, affected by the following factors:

- the appropriateness of team working for the particular organisational context (e.g. task interdependence, culture/structure/technology)
- the design of team working (e.g., the model of team working selected by the organisation)
- implementation factors (e.g., management commitment, degree of employee participation, time/resources invested)

Essentially, these are factors that affect whether the implementation of team working has any 'bite'; that is, whether or not it leads to any positive and sustained change in work characteristics. Each of these categories of factors is described in turn.

6.3.2 The organisational context within which team working is introduced

An initial set of factors that affect whether team working has a positive effect on work design concerns the context within which team working is introduced. Organisational context refers to aspects of the organisational environment in which the team operates (e.g. the level of task interdependence, the structure, technology used, etc.). Team working is unlikely to be successful within some organisational contexts. Yet in other settings team working can operate successfully. We describe here two contextual factors that are important for team working:

- some degree of task interdependence
- organisational 'readiness' for team working

a) Some degree of task interdependence

The appropriateness of teams in the first place will depend on how interdependent the tasks are. That is, it is important that team working is not implemented in situations that are not suited to such a way of working just because it is seen as 'the thing to do'. One important pre-condition for effective team working is interdependence, that is, the degree to which employees need to collaborate to achieve their goals. If interdependence is low, the value of team working is likely to be lower, and could even be detrimental. Several researchers have reported a lack of interdependence as a factor that contributes to the failure of team working initiatives (Proctor & Mueller, 2000); Pearce & Ravlin, 1987; Cohen & Ledford, 1994). In addition, where team working has been implemented in low interdependence settings the benefits of team working have been found to be minimal (Sprigg, Jackson & Parker, 2000; Liden, Wayne & Bradway, 1995).

As an example, Sprigg, Jackson & Parker (2000) investigated the implementation of team working in a wire and rope manufacturing company. In the company, wire makers had less interdependence than rope makers and it was found that the wire makers also had lower mental health and performance than the rope makers. Further, the lower reported levels of well-being and performance in the wire makers was found to be due to their low interdependence. This study therefore illustrates that implementing team working into a production setting that is low in work interdependence (i.e., unsuitable for team working) can lead to detrimental effects on effectiveness.

Study 1 in this report adds support to this finding. In one area of the company team working was found not to exist despite having been implemented. A detailed examination of the context showed that this particular area was not suited to team-based working. Not only were the teams spread over such a large area that working together was very difficult, but the team members did not need each other in order to get their job done (i.e., they had low interdependence). If team members did help their team mates, their own productivity was likely to be reduced because they could not simultaneously watch their own machine. The lack of interdependence was suggested as a factor that reduced the effectiveness of team working in this area. However, in addition to being unsuccessful, the team working initiative was actually detrimental to employee well-being. After the failed implementation, the employees in this area were more stressed than they had been prior to the initiative (*see Study 1, Section 7, for a detailed description of this finding).*

It is therefore critical that companies accurately assess whether team working is an appropriate form of work design. Team working is appropriate if there is some value in employee co-operating together, such as by sharing information and resources. If there is little value in such co-operation, then team working should not be implemented (or interdependence should be increased prior to implementing teams; see next). Other options that could be explored as a means of increasing flexibility include off-the-job improvement teams, job enrichment and suggestion schemes.

Another option is that organisations can explicitly seek to increase the interdependence between the tasks prior to introducing team working, such as by introducing cellular manufacturing (i.e. the grouping of machines, people, and processes into 'cells' where a particular product or type of product is made) or introducing shared goals that explicitly require co-ordination across the team.

b) Organisational readiness for team working

The wider organisational context and culture in which team working is introduced should be considered when designing the model of team working that is to be adopted (Morgeson, Aiman-Smith & Campion, 1997; Mueller, 1994). If the structure and culture are highly bureaucratised (as in a traditional mechanistic organisation), then the implementation of a team-based structure, especially a self-managing team structure, is likely to be fraught with difficulty. For example, if managers in the organisation are used to operating in a traditional control-oriented way, then it will be very difficult for them to support a transition to self-managed working.

There are practical guidelines that assess an organisations' 'readiness for teams', such as that by Wellins *et al.,* (1991, p.95-97). An illustration of the types of guidelines that Wellins *et al* suggest are:

- employees should be able to suggest and implement improvements to their work area without going through several levels of approval
- the technology should be flexible enough to permit restructuring or reorganisation based on the needs of the teams
- management in the organisation should be willing to adjust responsibility downwards and radically change their own roles and behaviour

This selection of items in the 'readiness for teams' survey shows the types of culture and practices required for a receptive response to teams (a high score means the organisation is more ready).

For example, there is no point in trying to implement self-managed team working on an assembly line where the employee has no opportunity to alter how and when they do their tasks. In addition, if the organisation is very mechanistic and bureaucratic, with a great many levels of hierarchy, self-managing teams are unlikely to succeed without rather radical structural changes.

In large part, the lack of 'organisational readiness' for team working was a reason that it was not successful within the production area described in Study 1. The organisation was very traditional, with a strong culture of hierarchical decision-making and managerial control.

Box 11 summarises the important contextual factors to consider when deciding on whether to embark on team working.

Box 11: Organisation context factors to consider when contemplating team working

- Some degree of interdependence between group members' tasks
- A culture and structure that is 'ready' for team working

6.3.3 The design of team working

When organisations embark on team working, there are several design decisions that need to be made, including:

a) the size and scope of the team
b) the degree of employee self management intended in the team
c) the model of supervision

a) Size and scope of the team

A team should constitute a 'logical' task grouping, in which there is a clear boundary between the group's work and the work of others. For this reason, team working often involves re-organising work into, for example, product-based cells in which all of the people, technology and skills required to make a whole product (e.g. a particular car seat) are grouped together, rather than the more traditional functional form of organisation (e.g. all the assemblers work together, all of the quality personnel are grouped together, and so on). The team usually involves a manageable number of people (10-12 is usually considered the upper limit). Study 2 shows how larger-sized teams (some with as many as 20 people) were less effective than smaller-sized teams.

The team should also have clear shared goals that cover a number of aspects (e.g. customer satisfaction, quality, efficiency).

b) Degree of employee self-management in the team

A self-managing team design is the most likely to result in enhanced employee well being. Based on socio-technical systems theory, a recommendation is that the team should have sufficient autonomy to plan and manage all aspects of their own work. This includes responsibility for the following types of activities:

- setting goals, planning & scheduling
- allocating work amongst group members
- deciding on work methods
- obtaining and evaluating measures of work performance
- selecting and training group members

Further description of the self-managing team model is given in Section 5.2.

Study 2 describes the introduction of lean teams, which by virtue of their focus on standardised processes, are unlikely to enhance job autonomy and might even decrease it. Therefore, organisations contemplating the introduction of team working need to be made aware that there are different models of team working, and that the model they choose could dramatically affect team working's success and its impact on employee well-being.

c) Model of supervision

An important aspect relating to the model of team working concerns the choices made regarding the style and structure of supervision. Many researchers have noted that supervisory style can contribute to the failure of team working initiatives (e.g., Cummings, 1978; Klein, 1984; Letize & Donovan, 1990; Manz & Sims, 1987; Walton & Schlesinger, 1979). For example, Cohen, Ledford & Speitzer (1996) found that whilst supervision did not affect effectiveness within traditional work teams, it was actually detrimental within self-managing teams. In addition, Beekun (1989) found in a meta-analysis of studies of team effectiveness, that teams with supervision performed worse than those who operated without supervision.

A principle reason for the latter finding is the reluctance of supervisors to relinquish control to team members (e.g., Manz & Sims, 1987), which results in teams not having the autonomy that they need to solve problems effectively. This is illustrated in Case C, which showed that one of the main barriers to the development of self-managed team working, was managers' taking a "controlling" supervision style. In order for self-managed teams to actually organise their own work, managers need to relinquish decision-making to the teams.

It is also critical that if the model of team working is one in which there are traditional supervisors or hands-on team leaders, efforts must be made to ensure the supervisor/team leader does not simply act in the traditional directing and controlling way. Indeed, this is probably one of the greatest risks associated with the team leader model – that the team leader will simply take on the responsibilities previously held by the supervisor, and will not distribute them to all team members.

The above situation was shown to have occurred in several studies reported by Parker, Jackson, Sprigg & Whybrow (1998) where team *leaders* were found to have more enriched jobs and better mental health than team members but there was little positive impact of team working on the jobs of team *members*. Similarly, Study 3 showed that the full benefits of self-managing team working can only be achieved if a large number of team members take on self-managing responsibilities. When just one or two members do not, the effects of the implementation of team working are less beneficial. Companies must therefore ensure that all team members, not just the team leaders, are encouraged and trained to take on self-managing responsibilities.

Study 2 showed that the most successful lean teams were those in which participants had a high degree of influence over decisions rather than decision making being dominated by the supervisor or the engineer.

Some researchers argue that even self-managing teams need some form of supervision within the team (e.g., Ilgen, Major, Hollenbeck & Sego, 1993). This leadership can take varying forms (Kogler Hill, 1997). For example, there can be a designated team leader, the team leader role can be rotated periodically between members of the team, or the leadership role can be shared amongst team members. However, regardless of how such leadership takes place, it is important that the team obtains support and direction from the leader *without the leader acting in a controlling and directive role.*

A key role of someone who manages a self-managing team will be "boundary management", in which the individual liaises with other teams and other departments to ensure the group has the necessary resources. Managers typically need training in this role.

Box 12 summarises the considerations that need to be made when designing team working.

Box 12: Designing an effective team

- The team should: be based around a logical group of tasks, have shared goals, and should contain no more than 10 -12 members
- The team should be designed so that the team members have sufficient autonomy to manage day-to-day team activities
- The style and structure of supervision should help spread self-management throughout the team

6.3.4 Implementation factors

The literature on organisational change documents many factors that affect the implementation of a change initiative. Here, we describe some of the factors that we believe are particularly important for the successful implementation of team working. These are summarised in Box 13.

Box 13: Factors that enhance the successful implementation of team working

- A clear strategy for implementing team working
- Management commitment to team working
- Realistic expectations and a long-term approach to implementation
- Sufficient resources allocated to team working, especially for training
- Stakeholder involvement and participation in the design & implementation process
- Alignment of wider organisational and human resource systems (e.g., training, payment, reward, information systems) with team working

- **A clear strategy for implementing team working**

  The strategy driving the implementation of team working is likely to impact on the nature of team working and its work design consequences. There are two aspects:

  - What are the strategic reasons for implementing team working?
  - How clearly articulated are those reasons?

For example, regarding the former, if team working is being introduced simply as a way of short-term cost cutting, then the focus will probably be on the cost savings arising from removing supervisors. In such a scenario, it is unlikely the organisation will take the necessary steps to empower teams and team members. Likewise, if the strategy behind team working is primarily to achieve standardisation of processes (as in the company reported in Study 2), the company is unlikely to put resources and effort into enhancing employee self-management.

Similarly, if there is no clearly articulated strategy – and team working is mostly being introduced 'because competitors are doing it' – then it is unlikely that team working will have much of an impact because the necessary resources will not be put into implementation. In Study 1, team working was more successful and long-lasting within the maintenance area than in production area. Within the maintenance area, there was a very clearly articulated strategy regarding team working. The goals of team working were stated in written and verbal forms. Within the production area, in contrast, it was much more unclear for those involved as to why team working was being implemented.

- **Management commitment to team working**

  A factor that has been repeatedly identified as important for successful change is management commitment to the new initiative, and team working is no exception. One of the major differentiating factors that explained the relative success of team working in maintenance compared to production (Study 1) is management commitment. Managers in maintenance were committed to team working right from the outset, putting in long hours beyond their normal job hours to make it work (*see* Case 5, Parker *et al.,* 1998). The key manager driving team working remained in the position throughout the study period. In contrast, the managers in production, although by their own report were committed to team working, in fact focused much more on other issues (e.g., individual machine productivity). There was also more turnover and restructuring amongst the management group that made it hard to develop continuity in team working efforts.

- **Realistic expectations and a long-term approach to implementation**

  If management do not realise that developing teams is a lengthy, time-consuming and labour-intensive process (Wellins *et al.,* 1991), then it is likely they will be disappointed with team working. Sustained and continuous effort is needed. It is also of paramount importance that team working is developed beyond the period of implementation. A danger that many companies fall into is that they think the job is done once team working has been launched. However, as Parker & Wall (1998) observed, the implementation of work redesign should be considered an evolving process that requires considerable learning and adjustment. Mohrman *et al.,* (1995) similarly argued that new forms of team-based work organisations cannot be achieved by a "one-shot implementation" (p.31), but will be a gradual transition involving many years.

Once teams are physically in place and operating in their new form of working, it is necessary to develop and train the teams so that the optimum benefits can be gained. Study 1 is a good illustration of this point. In one part of the company (production), teams were implemented, but thereafter there was little or no emphasis by managers on team working. However, in another part of the company (maintenance), managers spent considerable time and effort developing the teams and seeking ways to improve team working. Although both areas saw benefits of team working in the short term, in the long term only the teams that had been continually developed were still successful operating in teams.

- **Sufficient time and personnel resources allocated to team working, especially for training**

There is a mistaken view that the implementation of initiatives like team working do not require many resources. In terms of large amounts of capital, this is reasonably true, at least compared to the purchasing and installation of many types of technology. However, the effective implementation of team working requires considerable resources, particularly in terms of personnel time (e.g., the time spent by management developing teams, the time spent by employees in training, etc.) and money for employee training (the cost of training per se and the cost of someone taking time out for training). If organisations are serious about implementing team working, they need to be prepared to allocate time and resources.

In Study 2, insufficient *time resources* were given to responding to lean team activities and requests. To progress their ideas for improvement, team members frequently needed the support of other departments and personnel to make the changes happen. For example, the purchasing department needed to approve various decisions. However, this support and assistance was often not forthcoming, which was very demotivating for team members. The most effective teams were those who had greater support from other departments and their manager.

Training has been found to facilitate team working and team effectiveness, yet this is precisely the area in which many organisations fall down. Many organisations underestimate the degree of training required for employees to become more flexible and/or more self-managing. Training is important in terms of promoting technical skills to facilitate multiskilling, promoting greater knowledge of the organisation (its goals, competitors, processes etc), and ensuring employees have the necessary interpersonal and team working skills. For example, Study 3 showed that successful self-managed teams had a wider variety of different skills and had more flexibility amongst team members. It therefore appears that having the appropriate training for team members facilitates the development of self-managed team working.

Team leaders also need training. For example, a further differentiating factor between the success of team working within the maintenance area compared to production in Study 1 was that team leaders in maintenance were trained extensively but that team leaders in production received little or no training.

Another important resource is *information and information sharing.* Case C showed that a principal barrier to the development of self-managed teams was poor communication both within the team and between the team and day shift personnel. Therefore, in order for teams to work effectively they need to communicate well both within the team and they need to communicate well with others in the organisation.

- **Stakeholder involvement in the design and implementation process**

  A critical element of the relative success of a team working initiative has been found to be the way in which team working is implemented (Parker, Jackson, Sprigg & Whybrow, 1998; Tannenbaum, Salas & Cannon-Bowers, 1996; Badham, et al., 1996). All those who will be affected by team working (e.g. supervisors, managers, engineers, employees) should be involved in its design and implementation. In particular it is important to involve employees in the implementation process (Whybrow & Parker, 2000). For example, an investigation of team working in a wire manufacturing company found that the greatest individual benefits (i.e., lower stress and higher job satisfaction) and performance benefits (i.e., greater productivity, lower absence and accidents) occurred in those areas where employees were involved in the implementation of team working. Where employees were not involved in the process these effects were reduced (*see* Parker, Jackson, Sprigg & Whybrow, 1998, for a brief description of this see Study 1 in this report).

Involving employees in the implementation of team working is beneficial for several reasons. First, it utilises employees' expertise and thus facilitates the design of an appropriate form of team working (Whybrow & Parker, 2000; Heller, Pusic, Strauss & Wilpert, 1998). Better decisions are likely to be made about any work re-organisation because employees possess a great deal of tacit knowledge and local expertise. Second, participation enables an understanding of all stakeholders' reaction to the change (Parker & Axtell, 1998; Whybrow & Parker, 2000). Third, employee participation can increase employees' perceptions of fairness and can promote feelings of motivation towards and ownership over the change process (Kirkman & Sharpiro, 1999). Finally, involving employees in the process may reduce their resistance to the change (e.g., Dyer, 1987; Barker, 1993;; Manz & Sims, 1993; Osborn *et al.,* 1990). Kirkman & Sharpiro (1999) argued that resistance to team working is to be due to employees being concerned that they may have to take on undesirable tasks, that their workload will increase and that there will be a reduced effort from their team members. Further, Ezzamel & Willmolt (1998) suggested that resistance could be due to employees not wanting to take on what they see as 'management jobs'. By discussing team working with the employees and allowing team members to input their ideas about how team working could best be adopted, and how team working can be used to help address their work issues, it is likely that employees will feel greater commitment to the initiative and more positive and clear about why the initiative is happening. Study 1 in this report provides some evidence for this proposition since employees were more positive about team working in areas where team working had been successfully implemented.

- **Alignment of wider organisational and human resource systems with team working**

  Many researchers on team working point to the importance of aligning human resource practices to be consistent with the work design (e.g., Parker & Wall, 1998). For example, Hackman (1990) warned of the danger of calling a group of individuals a team but yet treating them and rewarding them as individual performers. This point is reiterated in Study 1 where in the production areas there was a heavy concentration on individual machine productivity. Such behaviour by managers makes it very difficult for teams to operate since helping a team mate an employee risks reducing their own performance (*see* Study 1 for a more detailed description of this issue). It is therefore important that the performance of teams is measured at the team level, and made available to the team, so that team members can focus on ensuring their overall team's production is maximised rather than purely focusing on their own part of the task.

Another human resource issue is the provision of feedback. Study 3 showed that some teams struggle to adopt self-managed team working because they are not told why their performance is lacking. Teams should therefore receive information about their team performance on a regular basis. Intuitively this makes sense because it is impossible for a team to improve itself and to effectively manage the day-to-day running of the team if they do not understand how well they are performing. Performance feedback should go beyond just letting teams know their overall performance. In particular it is important that feedback is specific so that teams know on what dimensions they particularly need to perform well.

More generally, teams should have access to all of the information needed to make autonomous decisions. For example, it is likely they will need information about supplies, customers, technologies, performance, and what is happening in other departments (e.g. planning, sales). Some redesign of information systems is therefore likely when implementing team working.

Other supporting changes also need to be made to human resource systems, such as introducing systems for providing and monitoring training, ensuring there are non-hierarchical career paths for team members and team leaders, and introducing payment systems that reward group-level performance. If changes are not made in these wider systems, it is unlikely that team working can be sustained. Study 1 illustrates how team working can fade if these types of broader changes are not made.

Box 14 (*see over)* shows some of the types of changes to human resource systems that are required to support self managing teams.

6.3.5 Summary of factors affecting the link between team working and work design

The implication of the above is very clear. If organisations want to implement team working in a way that positively impacts on work design, they need to:

- ensure that the context is task interdependent (i.e., that employees need to co-operate together to do their work). This might require changing and re-configuring tasks to enhance their interdependence.
- ensure that the organisational context and culture is conducive for team working
- design teams that are grouped around a logical set of tasks, and that are small enough to be manageable.
- design teams that allow group members sufficient autonomy to manage their daily activities
- develop a style and structure for supervision that is conducive to team member self-management.

Box 14: Human resource aspects required to support self-managing teams

(from Parker & Wall, 1998, p.126)

- Flexible and broad job descriptions
- Reward/grading system that promote appropriate behaviours (e.g., team-based pay)
- Systems to monitor and facilitate training
- The availability of non-hierarchical career paths
- Recruitment and selection systems based on appropriate criteria (e.g., preference for group working, trainability)
- Clear performance criteria/targets for the team
- Feedback and information systems that allow the team to act on problems that arise, make appropriate decisions, interact with other groups, and learn from their mistakes
- Layout of the work environment conducive to team working (team members near each other and somewhat separate from other teams)
- Modifications to technology to support enriched work roles

- clearly articulate the strategic intent behind team working
- attain and communicate management commitment to team working
- adopt a long term approach to the implementation of team working
- ensure that sufficient resources are allocated to team working (especially for training)
- involve employees in the implementation process
- align the wider organisational and human resource systems to team working (e.g., ensure teams have the information they need to make autonomous decisions; develop payment systems that promote team rather than individual performance).

6.4 CONDITIONS UNDER WHICH WORK DESIGN HAS A POSITIVE EFFECT ON WELL-BEING

6.4.1 Proposition 4: The effect of work design characteristics on well-being outcomes depends on various individual and contextual factors.

The relationship between work design and outcomes, or specifically the link between work characteristics (B) and well-being (C), has also been proposed to be dependent upon a number of factors (E). In other words, even if team working leads to enriched work design, there are some factors which affect whether and how strongly enriched work design leads to enhanced well-being (e.g., Parker & Wall, 1998; Wall & Jackson, 1995). A simple example is that some individuals do not want greater job autonomy, and therefore these individuals do not necessarily benefit from work enrichment.

Our aim in this section is not to review all possible contingency factors but rather, it is to point to some particularly pertinent ones that have been observed in the literature. For some factors (e.g., individual difference variables), there is specific evidence that they affect the link between work design and well-being. For other factors (e.g., uncertainty), the evidence applies more strongly to performance outcomes and we are speculating they could also affect the work design – well-being relationship.

6.4.2 Organisational context

At least two organisational context factors that are likely to affect the relationship between work design characteristics and well-being include:

- the level of operational uncertainty
- the existence of supportive human resource practices

- **Level of operational uncertainty**

  It has been found that the greater the degree of operational uncertainty (i.e., the more complex the situation), the more important it is for effective performance that the team is self-managing. Cordery, Wright & Wall (1997) investigated teams for 12 months before and 12 months after the introduction of autonomous work groups. They found that in work groups where there was little production uncertainty, there was little or no improvement in performance. However, as uncertainty increased the performance gains associated with the introduction of autonomy increased. Similar results have been found in relation to individual job autonomy. Thus, studies have shown that the performance gains associated with enhanced job autonomy are greatest in highly uncertain situations (e.g., Wall *et al.,* 1999).

Such research suggests that, in complex manufacturing where there is a high degree of uncertainty (e.g., as a result of frequently changing product designs, unreliable technology, changing market demands), self-managing teams will be the most effective form of team working and lean production teams will be inappropriate in such situations of high uncertainty. In situations where there is low uncertainty, it is likely that there will be little distinction between the effectiveness of different types of team for organisational gain. In fact one could speculate that the consistency of the standard operating procedures that are associated with lean production teams might even benefit productivity under conditions of low uncertainty. This does not mean to say, however, that lean production teams will necessarily be associated with better employee well-being. As described in Section 5.3, there is some evidence that 'lean' teams are indeed 'mean' teams.

Although we do not currently have the data to test this proposition in our own research, it is possible that one reason work design was more successful in the maintenance area of production (Study 1) is because this type of work is more complex and uncertain, with more scope for employees to benefit from greater decision-making, than the type of work performed by production operators making wire. Further research is needed to test this proposition.

- **Supportive human resource systems practices**

  As described above (*see* Section 6.3.3), for the implementation of team working to result in any actual change to job content, it is important to align various organisational and human resource practices with team working. It is similarly the case that, if human resource practices do not support enriched work design, then work design characteristics might not have the positive effects on well-being that are proposed. For example, for work redesign to be sustained, typically there needs to be a change in the payment system. It is commonly recommended, for example, that part of employees' payment be contingent on the acquisition and/or use of additional skills. Similarly, if employees decision-making responsibilities are expanded, yet they are not given the necessary training or information to make good decisions, then greater autonomy might not lead to the expected positive outcomes such as job satisfaction.

Box 15: Contextual factors that increase the positive effects of self management

- Uncertain, complex and dynamic settings
- Supportive human resource practices (e.g., adequate training, group based pay, dissemination of information to teams)

6.4.3 Individual difference factors

Individuals are also likely to vary in their response to work design characteristics (Hackman & Oldham, 1980; Parker & Wall, 1998). For example, it has been established that individuals who have higher levels of 'growth need strength' (i.e. an aspiration for growth and development) are more likely to respond to enriched work design (Hackman & Oldham, 1980). Similarly, drawing on the same data as reported in Study 1, Parker & Sprigg (1999) found that employees with a proactive personality were most likely to benefit in well-being terms from active jobs with high autonomy and moderate demands. In contrast, employees who were more naturally passive in their approach to problems did not appear to benefit particularly from enriched jobs.

Other individual difference factors could include: job security (those who have lower job security might react more negatively to work redesign), change orientation (employees who do not like change might resist work redesign), preference for group working/ collective orientation (those who prefer working in a group will respond more favourably to self managing teams), trust in management, and tolerance of role ambiguity (those who are able to tolerate ambiguity will respond better to enriched and less tightly defined work roles).

6.4.4 Leadership

As mentioned in Section 3.3.2, leadership within teams is a critical issue. Study 3 provides some interesting analyses that show how effective leadership can act in a compensatory role by motivating and inspiring employees to use their initiative when positive aspects of work design (e.g. autonomy) are lacking. This study suggests that, when it is not possible to increase the autonomy of a team, then their leaders can (if they adopt an effective style) help promote the use of personal initiative amongst team members.

6.5 SUMMARY, IMPLICATIONS AND SOME CAVEATS

6.5.1 Summary and implications

Based on our analysis of the literature and our research, we propose that the effect of team working on well-being depends to a large degree on how it affects work characteristics such as group levels of autonomy. Practical implications that arise from this are shown in Box 16.

Box 16: Recommendations for enriching work design when introducing team working

- For positive benefits of team working, the initiative must involve changes that will positively impact on work characteristics. For example, if team working is accompanied by an increase in team autonomy (i.e. greater self-management), then it is likely to lead to greater employee satisfaction and lower job stress.
- If team working is 'implemented' but no real and sustained effort is made to increase team members' autonomy, or enhance their involvement in decision-making, then team working is unlikely to have a positive impact on well-being.
- If team working has negative effects on work characteristics (such as the loss of job control associated with excessive standardisation of procedures), then it might well be accompanied by negative consequences for employees.
- To maximise the benefits of team working, organisations need to aim for it to be accompanied by the following work designs:
    - jobs in which employees have autonomy and involvement in decision-making
    - jobs with a variety of tasks (e.g., multiskilling)
    - meaningful work (e.g., working on a whole product or service rather than a fragmented part of the process
    - clear and consistent expectations about what is required of team members (i.e., no increase or decrease in levels of role conflict and role clarity)
- In cases where job autonomy is lowered because of standardisation of procedures (e.g., lean production teams), it is important that employees have some influence over the design of the procedures in the first place, and that they can continue to have influence over the procedures via group participation.

Despite the above recommendations, it is indeed quite common for team working to be implemented without it really affecting job content (each of the studies reported presents examples of this). We identified several factors that are likely to enhance the extent to which the implementation of team working leads to enriched work design. These are shown in Box 17.

Box 17: Factors that enhance team working effectiveness

- Introducing teams in an appropriate context
    - team working is suitable if there is some degree of task interdependence
    - the organisation needs to be 'ready' for team working (e.g., a non-authoritarian culture, non-hierarchical structure, coaching management style)
- An appropriate team work design
    - a team designed around a logical group of tasks
    - a manageable number of team members
    - a high degree of team self management
    - a style and structure of supervision that is conducive to self management spreading throughout the team
- Effective management of the implementation process
    - a clear strategy for team working that is articulated widely
    - strong management commitment to team working
    - realistic expectations and a long-term approach to implementation
    - sufficient resources allocated to team working, especially for training
    - employee involvement in the implementation process
    - alignment of human resource and other organisational practices with team working

Guidance follows quite straightforwardly from the above factors. For example, if there is no management commitment to team working, it is highly unlikely team working will be implemented successfully and therefore work content is unlikely to be changed. More generally, the point is that, by making appropriate informed choices, the organisation *can* intervene to reduce or prevent the psychosocial risks of team working that might occur, as well as maximise the possibility of mental health benefits.

The model also proposes that the link between work characteristics and well-being is affected by contextual and individual difference factors:

Box 18: Factors that enhance the positive consequences of enriched work characteristics

- Organisational context factors that enhance the positive consequences of self-management
    - a high level of operational uncertainty (the more uncertain and complex the task environment, the more likely enriched work design will lead to positive outcomes)
    - the existence of supportive HR practices (e.g., adequate training)
- Individual difference factors that are likely to enhance the positive consequences of self management
    - employee aspiration for growth and development (the higher the desire for growth and development, the more likely a positive response to work enrichment)
    - proactive personality (the more proactive the person, the more likely they will not be stressed by active jobs with high autonomy and moderate demands)
    - tolerance of role ambiguity (those able to tolerate ambiguity will also probably respond better to enriched and less tightly defined work roles)
    - other potential factors (e.g., job security, change orientation)
- Supportive coaching oriented leadership

The implications from the above are also quite straightforward. For example, work redesign will be most beneficial in complex and uncertain environments, and some individuals will respond more favourably to work redesign than others.

6.5.2 Some caveats about the model

Two important caveats about the proposed model of team working are as follows:

- There are potentially other ways in which team working might affect well-being.
  Our emphasis is on how *work characteristics* mediate the effect of team working on well-being outcomes. That is, we propose that team working will be more or less successful, depending on how it affects work characteristics such as job autonomy, social contact, and task variety. However, we are not suggesting that an impact on work characteristics is the

only way in which team working can have positive consequences for well-being. In particular, there is some evidence team working might result in changes to *group processes* (i.e. the way people work together, e.g., the level of team cohesion, the degree of communication) which can in turn affect well-being.

- The proposed model applied for particular types of teams.
  We looked at teams with specific characteristics (permanent membership, production teams, etc.), and the propositions might not apply to other sorts of teams.

6.5.3 Policy implications

In terms of policy, there are several implications that arise out of this research.

First it is important that the Health and Safety Executive continues to focus on employee well-being and mental health.

Second, it is important that health and safety inspectors and other HSE front-line representatives are trained to recognise work situations that might impinge on employee mental health and well-being, and to advise on sources of guidance for making improvements. For example, if inspectors observe that an organisation is implementing team working, they should be able to provide the organisation with advice on where they can obtain guidance on how to minimize its potential risks and maximise its benefits for employees.

Third, it is critical that training and guidance is provided to all those who are directly involved in implementing change that may have mental health implications for employees (e.g., human resource personnel, production managers, union representatives).

Fourth, it is important to recognise that the implementation of team working is not inevitably good for employee well being, nor is it inevitably bad. The effects of team working on well-being will depend on a number of organisational, design, strategic, individual, and implementation factors. The important point is that organisations recognise that they can make choices that have important consequences for well-being. Employers need to be fully informed about the choices available to them, and the consequences of these choices.

Finally, there is a need to continue to provide funding to enable researchers to discover more about mental health issues within organisations and how to manage them.

The combination of all these factors should help ensure that companies operate in ways that are not detrimental to the well-being of their employees, thus, optimising both employees lives and company effectiveness.

7. STUDY 1

A FOLLOW-UP OF THE IMPLEMENTATION OF TEAM WORKING WITHIN A BROWN FIELD MANUFACTURING SITE

7.1 SUMMARY

This case focuses on the implementation of 'flexible work teams' (i.e. teams in which a group of employees work together in a flexible way, with a team leader acting as a focal point for the team). Researchers tracked the effect of the transition from traditional working in which a large group of employees worked together under the supervision of a foreman to team-based working over a three-year period. Several important lessons can be learned from the relative success of the team working initiative in different areas of the company. First, it was found that implementing team working in a context unsuited for that form of work design was not only unsuccessful in performance terms, but was also detrimental to employees' well-being. Second, where team working was an appropriate form of work design, there were benefits for employees and for the organisation if employees were involved in the implementation process. Finally, in order for long-term benefits to be achieved, the implementation of team working needs to be a sustained and continued process of development.

7.2 THE SETTING

This case study reports on the implementation of team working in a brown field wire manufacturing company. In particular the focus here is on the move from individual to team-based working on the shop floor.

The current case is a follow up of two cases that we reported on in Parker, Jackson, Sprigg & Whybrow (1998) (*see* Cases 5 and 6). At the time of this original research team working had only been implemented within a maintenance function (*see* Case 5) and in one part of the production area (Case 6). Comparisons of those areas where there was team working with those areas where traditional working was still in operation showed some clear benefits of team working, both in terms of the well-being of employees and in terms of production, absenteeism and safety. However in the original report, it was also found that the way in which team working was implemented was of critical importance. The implementation of team working was more successful in areas where all team members were involved in the implementation process than in areas where only team leaders were involved in the process.

Since the researchers reported on this study, team working has been implemented within the remainder of the production workforce. The current study therefore investigates the effect of implementing team working in the area which had previously not had team working operating, and provides a follow up of those teams that were previously in existence to assess the long term effects of team working.

To set the scene for the current study, the history of team working and the findings from the earlier analysis are reviewed.

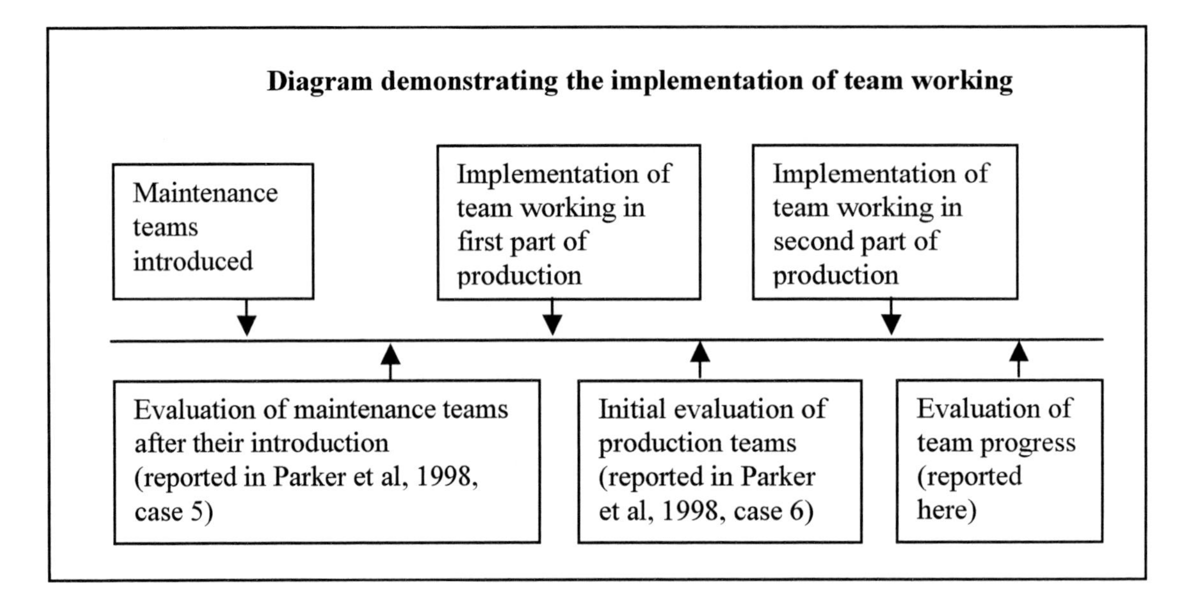

7.3 A RECAP ON THE HISTORY OF TEAM WORKING

7.3.1 Work design prior to team working

Prior to team working the employees had fairly traditional jobs with limited control over how and when they did tasks and limited variety in the type of tasks they conducted. For example, in the maintenance function, fitters fitted and electricians did electrical work whilst the foreman directed which jobs each individual was to do, in what order they were to do them, and how they were to do them. Similarly in production, one employee was responsible for running a certain set of machines and each employee always worked on these same machines.

In the early to mid 1990s, pressures from the parent company and competitors led to redundancies and major structural and organisational changes (e.g. the introduction of total quality management procedures) at this company. In addition, management recognised that their employees were not very flexible. It was therefore decided to introduce 'flexible work groups', as one manager said "to release the latent potential in our workforce".

The team working initiative was first piloted in the smaller maintenance function. Team working was then implemented within part of production. It was after this that our first evaluation took place. Since then the final area of production has implemented team working.

The different timing in the implementation of team working and the different level of involvement of the employees meant that we could make comparisons between different groups of teams. The only difference in the implementation of team working between the areas was the fact that in one of the production areas all team members (rather than just team leaders) were involved in the implementation of team working. In our previous reporting of the case these were called 'high flying teams' because they had better work design and higher levels of well-being amongst team members. In the area where team working was implemented with only the involvement of team leaders, we called the teams 'developing teams' since team working was in operation but it was not as successful as in the 'high flying teams'. Where team working had not been implemented, we described the area as 'traditional' working. Finally, the implementation of team working in the maintenance function was reported in a separate case in the Parker, Jackson, Sprigg & Whybrow (1998) report. We therefore simply refer to these as 'maintenance teams'.

7.4 DIFFERENCES BETWEEN TYPES OF TEAM AT THE FIRST EVALUATION

7.4.1 The beneficial effect of team working

As can be seen from Figure 1, at Phase 1, the fundamental difference was that those employees who worked in teams had more enriched work designs, more commitment to team working, better team functioning and better mental health than those employees who had the traditional individual-based working.

7.4.2 Importance of team member involvement

In addition, there was a noticeable advantage of having involved all team members in the implementation of team working. In particular the high-flying teams (in which all team members had been involved) reported having greater team autonomy and better team functioning than the maintenance and developing teams (in which only team leaders had been involved) (*see* Figure 1).

Interestingly team working was going remarkably well in the maintenance department even though the team members hadn't been involved in the implementation process. In fact their scores revealed that on many attributes they were on a par with the high-flying teams. In particular there was no difference between maintenance and highflying teams in terms of job control, job satisfaction and job security. On some attributes, the scores of the maintenance teams actually exceeded those of the high-flying teams. This was the case for role breadth, task variety, trust in team-mates, team efficacy and organisational commitment.

There are two possible reasons for the relative success of team working in the maintenance department. It may be that because the teams had been operating for longer in this area the teams had had a greater chance to develop and gain benefits from team working. Alternatively it could be that maintenance jobs were more suited to team working, or because of the methods of implementing team working within this area were more effective. We discuss this further later.

In terms of the issue of involvement of team members in the process, it is interesting to compare the high-flying to the developing teams since these two types of teams both work in the production area. It was found that the high-flying teams had greater team autonomy, lower workload, higher team efficacy, better team functioning, higher job satisfaction, and a higher opinion of management than the developing teams. This suggests that there is an advantage of involving all team members in the process of implementing team working.

7.5 CHANGES INTRODUCED SINCE FIRST EVALUATION

Since the first evaluation, the major change that occurred within production was that team working was introduced in the traditional working area. Showing a failure to learn lessons from the previous evaluation, only team leaders were involved in the process of implementing teams. Moreover, although team working was supposedly a priority for management, the production areas managers have had little to do with the teams and have not given much attention to team working. Rather, their concentration has been largely on developing standard operating procedures and increasing individual machine productivity. This lack of concentration of team working within production is evidenced by several comments we received:

- *" .... everything is about man per hour tonnage now ... "*
- *" Since team working started I feel it has declined in value quite a lot ... "*
- and even a manager commented *" Team working has not been moved forward over the last couple of years ... "*

Figure 3 : Differences between types of team at time 1

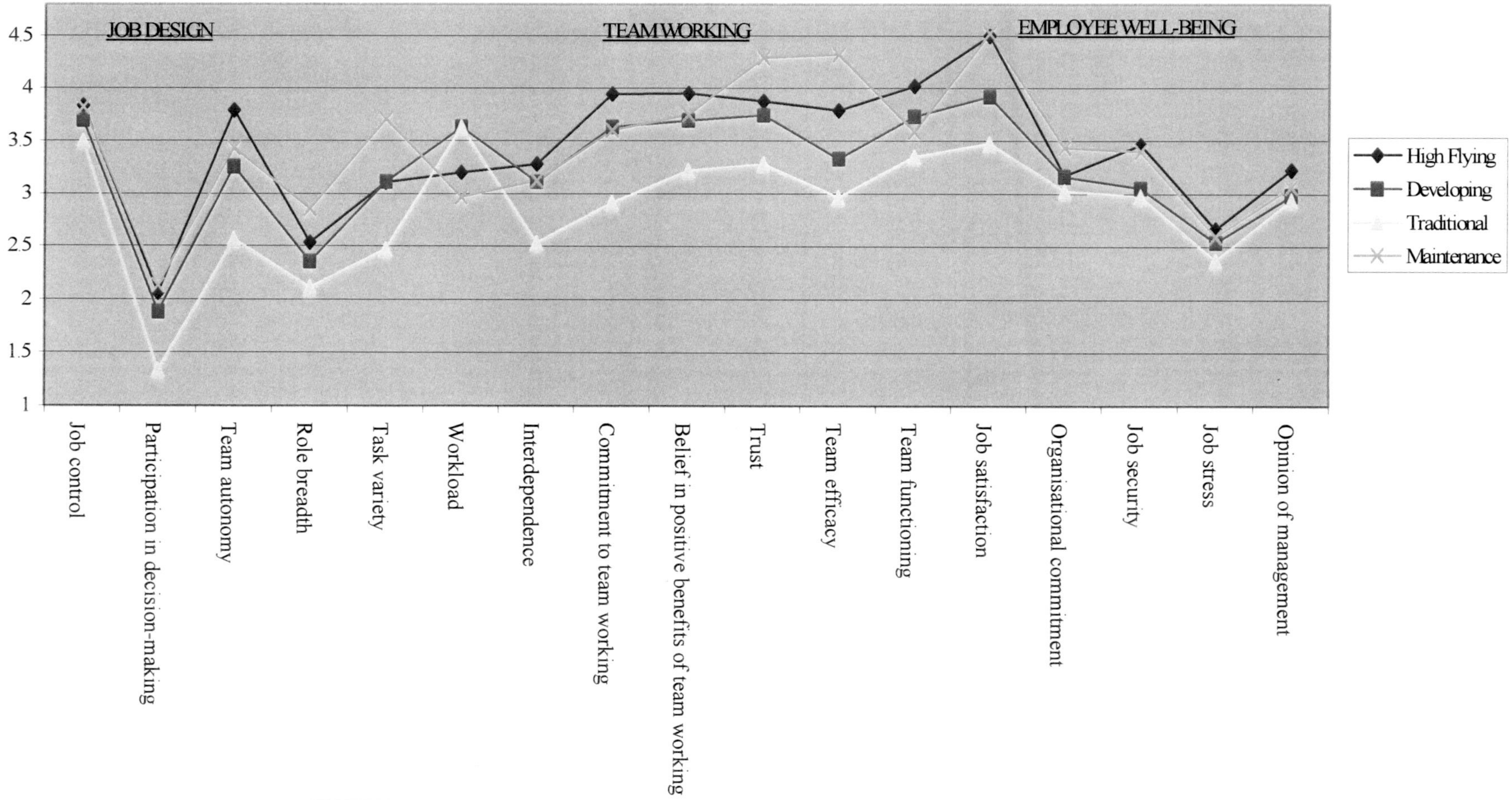

JOB DESIGN
TEAM WORKING
EMPLOYEE WELL-BEING

4.5
4
3.5
3
2.5
2
1.5
1

Job control
Participation in decision-making
Team autonomy
Role breadth
Task variety
Workload
Interdependence
Commitment to team working
Belief in positive benefits of team working
Trust
Team efficacy
Team functioning
Job satisfaction
Organisational commitment
Job security
Job stress
Opinion of management

High Flying
Developing
Traditional
Maintenance

All results are shown in terms of a 5-point scale where 1 = low, and 5 = high

Within maintenance, the major change was that there were redundancies in the maintenance function. In order to create a smooth downsizing in the maintenance department, the managers in this area spent considerable time and effort working with the teams to make improvements and have communicated clearly and frequently with all employees about issues and developments in their area.

The table below summarises the state of team working development at the two principal research phases:

Summary of the implementation of team working at the two principle research phases			
Maintenance teams	**High flying teams**	**Developing teams**	**Traditional working**
First Evaluation			
Team working implemented as a pilot for the site. Only team leaders were involved in the process.	Team working implemented. All team members were involved in the process.	Team working implemented. Only team leaders were involved in the process.	Team working not yet implemented.
Second Evaluation			
Work conducted on developing the teams and in communicating openly with all employees.	No proactive concentration on team working by management.	No proactive concentration on team working by management.	Team working implemented since Phase 1. Only team leaders were involved in the process. Followed by a period where managers concentrated little on team working.

7.6 IMPACT OF CHANGES

There are two particularly interesting ways to look at the data from the second evaluation:

- investigating differences between the types of teams in terms of their work design, team functioning and employee well-being at the second time point.
- examining the changes that have taken place over time within each of the types of teams.

These analyses are reported in turn.

7.7 DIFFERENCES BETWEEN THE TYPES OF TEAM WITHIN THE SECOND EVALUATION

In the second evaluation we found a completely different pattern of results (*see Figure 2*) than that found in the first evaluation. Most noticeably there was no longer much distinction between the different types of production teams. In fact, the only significant differences found between the types of production teams are that:

- there is a higher belief in the positive benefits of team working in the developing teams than in the traditional and high-flying teams
- the high flying teams have a higher opinion of management than the developing and traditional teams
- that the traditional teams have lower organisational commitment and job security than the developing and high-flying teams

There are therefore far fewer differences between the types of production teams at Phase 2 than at Phase 1. As we describe later, this is primarily because of a decline within the highflying teams.

7.8 THE IMPORTANCE OF CONTINUAL TEAM WORKING DEVELOPMENT

The real distinction at this second time point is between the maintenance teams and the production teams. The maintenance teams had more enriched jobs, more positive beliefs about team working, better team functioning, greater job satisfaction and lower job related stress than all the types of production teams. These results suggest that over time the method of implementing team working has become unimportant. In addition, the area in which team working is thriving is the area in which team-working has been continually developed since implementation. This suggests that team working cannot be implemented and then forgotten. Rather the implementation of team working needs to be a long-running and continued initiative.

In order to better understand why the distinctions have disappeared between the different types of production teams and why the maintenance teams are thriving the next section examines how things have changed within each of the types of teams.

Figure 2; Differences between types of team at time 2

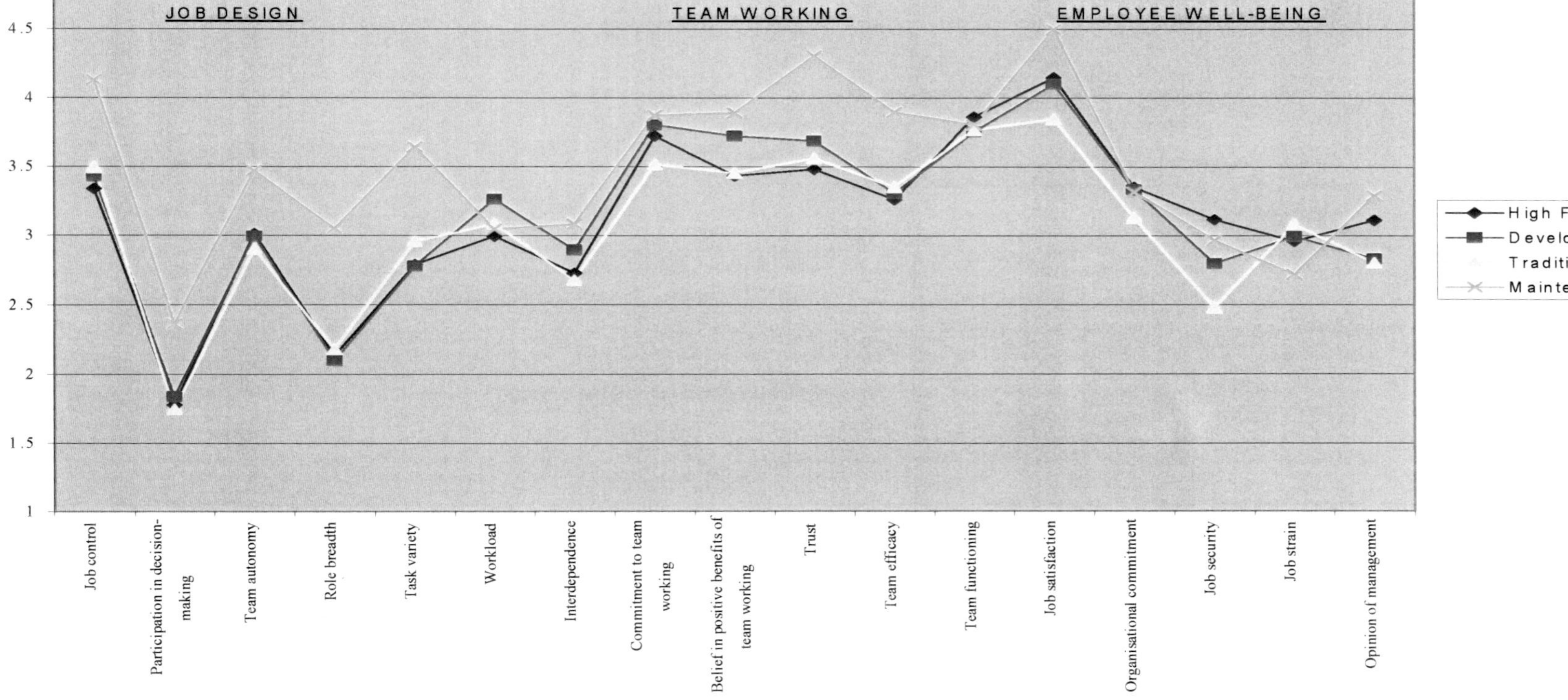

All results are shown in terms of a 5-point scale where 1 = low, and 5 = high

7.9 DIFFERENCES BETWEEN THE DIFFERENT TYPES OF TEAMS OVER TIME

7.9.1 Change over time within the high-flying teams

As mentioned above, since phase 1 there has been little concentration on team working in the production areas where team working had already been introduced. Instead the managers have concentrated on developing standard operating procedures and increasing individual machine productivity. Analyses comparing team members' scores at phase 2 with those at phase 1 (*see* Table 5) have found that within the high-flying teams there has been a decline in work design with team members reporting less control, less team autonomy, less role breadth, lower work load, and less interdependence between members of the team. This decline in the enrichment of team members' jobs suggests that there is less team working happening in the high flying areas than there was at Phase 1. Since the concentration has been on standard operating procedures and the optimisation of individual machine efficiency this result is perhaps unsurprising. The general pattern of decline is also seen in terms of team working. In particular members of the high flying teams are less positive about team working, have less trust in their team mates and are less confident about their teams ability than they were in phase 1.

On a positive note this decline in job enrichment and team working does not appear to have affected employee well being, although there has been no improvement in either well-being or mental health (e.g. their levels of job satisfaction, job stress and organisational commitment remain about the same as in the phase 1 evaluation). These results therefore suggest that the advantage gained by involving team members at the stage of implementing team working is lost if teams are not continually developed. In fact, the results go as far as to suggest that, in this company, team working has all but disappeared when no attention is given to building and developing the teams.

7.9.2 Changes over time within the developing teams

As with the high flying teams there has been little or no effort to improve team working since it was implemented and there has been concentration on standard operating procedures and individual machine productivity. A comparison of the scores of team members at phase 1 and at phase 2 (see table 1) show that there has been a decline in work design in the developing teams. In particular team members were found to have less participation in decision-making, a narrower role, less task variety, lower workload and less interdependence with their team-mates than at phase 1. Interestingly though, there was found to be no change in team working, the degree of job stress that team members experience was however found to have increased.

As with the high flying teams we therefore also find a trend of decline within the developing teams and this is likely to be because team working has not been developed since it was implemented. However, it appears that the decline is less pronounced than in the high-flying teams. This is probably because these developing teams exhibited less team working than the highflying teams shortly after implementation. The developing teams therefore had less far to fall than the high flying teams who were relatively successful at phase 1, and also the expectations in the developing area were not as high as in the high-flying area because only team leaders had been involved in the implementation process.

7.9.3 Change over time within traditional teams

In the traditional area team working was supposedly implemented in the time between the two research time points. We would therefore have expected there to be quite a bit of change within this area. The results however show that this is not the case (see table 1). In terms of job design the only difference is in the workload that team members have and this change was evidenced in both the other production areas. The fact that there has been no change in autonomy, participation, task variety and interdependence suggests that team working had not been successfully implemented in this area. Comments from team members illustrate that team working, although attempted, is not operating in this area. When asked about team working in their area team members commented *"team working is non-existent"*, *"it's not working" and "there is no team working"*.

The fact that team working does not exist despite having been apparently implemented may explain the fact that job stress has increased and job security has decreased in this area. Trying to implement team working but not succeeding is likely to be both stressful and demoralising to team members.

A more detailed look at the traditional teams suggests why team working has not been successfully adopted in this area. Essentially it appears that the area is not suitable for team based working. This is primarily because the operators work too far apart to be able to work together. For instance in one team they physically can't see one of the team members because the machines that that team member operates are in a separate area of the factory. In addition, in this traditional area there are more machines than there are men (for example 4 operators to 8 machines). This means that each operator is responsible for running a certain number of machines. There is therefore no interdependence between team members and this situation is exacerbated by the fact that there is a heavy concentration by management on individual machine productivity. Therefore if a team member spends time helping another team member who is experiencing problems with his/her machines the team member that is helping out will not produce as much during their shift and they will therefore not reach the targets set for their machines. These issues arose frequently in the interviews we conducted in this area. For example one team member said *" all we can do is keep (our) machines running as best we can"* and another commented that *" team working may be OK in small areas, but try walking up and down a shop 80-100 metres long all day".*

It therefore appears that team working was not suitable within this production area. The fact that job stress increased suggests that attempting to implement team working in an area not suited to that form of working, not only doesn't work, but also is potentially detrimental to the mental health of the employees.

7.9.4 Change over time within maintenance teams

The pattern of effects is remarkably different in the maintenance area than within the production areas. Comparisons of maintenance employees' reports at phase 1 from those at phase 2 show that there has been no change in the work design in this area. However, team members report having more trust in one another and their confidence in their teams ability has increased. There also appears to be better team functioning in this area than there was at phase 2. In terms of employee well-being, there has also been found to be improvements over time, with team members reporting greater job satisfaction and more positive opinions of management than they did at phase 1. In fact the only detrimental effect that has occurred over time in the maintenance function is that the team members feel they have less job security than they did in phase 1. Given the fact that there have been fairly large-scale redundancies in this area this is unsurprising. In fact, with such downsizing having taken place it is remarkable that a reduction in feelings of job security is the only detrimental change that has occurred.

The results within the maintenance function are therefore very positive and suggest that, not only is team based working still very much in operation, but also the way in which the teams operate has improved. In addition, job satisfaction has improved in this area. This improvement, which is not evident in any of the other areas in the company, is likely to be due at least in part to the considerable time and effort that managers in this area have spent in helping the teams to improve and in communicating clearly and frequently with all employees. The results from the maintenance teams therefore clearly suggest that it is beneficial for teams to be developed beyond the period of the implementation of team working.

A further factor that likely to have enhanced the success of team working in maintenance is that team working was implemented with a very solid base. Right from the beginning, effort was made to align wider systems (e.g. payment structures, working patterns) with team working and a great deal was invested in aspects such as team leader training (see Case 5, Parker, Jackson, Sprigg & Whybrow, 1998).

7.10 SUMMARY OF FINDINGS

An investigation of changes over time has therefore shown that in both the high-flying and developing areas team working has deteriorated. In the traditional area an attempt to implement team working appears to have failed, and within this area employees reported greater stress and insecurity, suggesting that failed initiatives may be detrimental to employee mental health. However, in the maintenance department, where efforts have been made to continually develop team working, there has been improvement. The results therefore highlight the importance of following through with team development beyond the period of implementation. It is not sufficient to just take the time to install team working, there also needs to be a continuous emphasis on improving and developing the teams. These results also explain the different patterns of results found at phase 1 and phase 2. At time 1 there were clear differences between the production areas where team working had been implemented and where it had not. However, at phase 2, few of these differences still existed. Since very little change over time had occurred in the traditional area (where team working hadn't been implemented at phase 1) this suggests that the production teams have lost all the benefits of team working that they had gained by the original implementation of team working.

In addition, the distinction between those teams where all team members were involved in the process of implementation and those where only team leaders were involved was also not evident at phase 2. Again this suggests that without continued work on team working the distinct advantage of involving teams in the implementation process does not last. Finally, the results from the traditional area suggest that team working does not exist even though it was implemented. A detailed examination of the context in this area suggests that this failure was due partly to the fact that team working is not a viable form of work design in this area. There was little or no interdependence between team members, too great a geographical area in which the teams were expected to operate, and too great an emphasis on individual productivity. At the same time, there was little support from management in terms of making team working effective.

7.11 LESSONS LEARNED

Three major implications can be drawn from this case study:

- team working should not be implemented in areas where the context is not suited to that form of work design. Team working requires a context in which there is interdependence, and a work layout that enables team members to communicate and work together. If it is implemented in an inappropriate setting, it not only doesn't work, it can also be detrimental to the well-being of the employees.
- involving team members in the implementation of team working is beneficial in the short term (both for employees and for the organisation). However, without follow up and continued development the beneficial effects are unlikely to last in the long term.
- the implementation of team working only succeeds in the long term if the teams are continually developed beyond the implementation process. Some ways in which teams can continue to be developed include regular meeting to discuss how the team could improve and continued team training.
- team working will not be successful with only a structural change (e.g., the removal of supervisors and the introduction of team leaders). This is especially true within an organisation such as the one described in this case that has a long history of simplified shop floor jobs and hierarchical decision making. A great deal of effort and commitment needs to go into team working in order to restructure and design the new work processes.
- team working cannot be successfully implemented without an investment of resources (e.g., training, management time, employee time).

Figure 5: Change over time for each of the different types of team				
	High flying teams	**Developing teams**	**Traditional working**	**Maintenance teams**
JOB DESIGN				
Job Control	↓			
Participation in Decisions		↓		
Team Autonomy	↓			
Role Breadth	↓			
Task Variety		↓		
Work Load	↓	↓	↓	
Interdependence	↓	↓		
TEAM WORKING				
Views about benefits of team working	↓			
Trust	↓			↑
Team Efficacy	↓			↑
Team Functioning				↑
EMPLOYEE WELL-BEING				
Job Satisfaction				↑
Organisational Commitment		↑		
Job Security			↓	↓
Job Stress		↓	↓	
Opinion of Management				↑

8. STUDY 2

CASE TRUCKER (PART B): THE NEED FOR PARTICIPATIVE DESIGNS AND A SUPPORTIVE ENVIRONMENT WHEN INTRODUCING EARLY STAGE LEAN PRODUCTION TEAMS

8.1 SUMMARY

One form of team working that is popular in vehicle manufacturing is the 'lean' production team. A preliminary form of lean teams were introduced within Company Trucker. The lean teams involved groups of employees analysing, improving and standardising production processes. Researchers tracked the effect of implementing lean teams over a three year period. Looking at the effects of lean teams for all teams combined, the researchers concluded that there was a small positive benefit for employees' jobs and well-being. However, more detailed analyses showed that the quality of teams and their impact varied. Members of teams in which there was little opportunity to participate in making team-related decisions, and in which supervisors, managers, and other departments did not actively support the team's activities, reported negative job changes (e.g. reduced method control), increased depression and reduced job satisfaction. The study suggests that there will be little added value of lean teams if they are not designed well and supported appropriately. Indeed such teams can be damaging to employee morale and well-being. Supervisors have a key role to play in developing and supporting teams.

8.2 THE SETTING

The case study was carried out in a UK-based manufacturing company. There were about 800 employees and the workforce was growing. This case study focuses on production employees, of whom there were approximately 500.

During the period of the research, a multinational US organisation took over the family-owned company. The senior management team, comprising a mixture of UK and US managers, began to implement a mixture of mass production and lean production principles within the organisation. One of the changes the company introduced was a moving assembly line in one area of production. An analysis of this change over an 18 month period showed that the moving line had large negative effects on the quality of jobs and the well-being of employees who were involved (see Case Trucker Part A; Parker, Jackson, Sprigg & Whybrow, 1998). The current case focuses on production employees who were not involved in the moving line, but who were involved in a related change, the implementation of an early form of lean production teams. The current study spans a period of three years.

Other changes that were on-going over the three year period included:

- increased outsourcing and a tighter focus on core business
- capital expenditure to improve physical work conditions
- changes in personnel procedures to align with corporate practices
- the introduction of 'planned methods' involving the simplification of work processes, facilitated by a recently created Technical Resources department
- initiatives to design products for manufacturability (e.g., engineers working more closely with operators to make parts that required 'assembly' only rather than 'fitting').

There was also an increase in the number of vehicles being produced per day, leading to the recruitment of a large temporary work force to help meet the additional demands.

8.3 PRE-LEAN TEAMS

Before the implementation of the early form of lean teams, what was the design of work for production employees and were there any stress risks for these employees? A survey was conducted to assess the situation. The survey results were compared with those from other manufacturing companies.

Most production employees worked in traditional work groups, with a supervisor who directed their work activities. On the whole, work loads were reasonable and employees were not excessively pressured. Most (81%) were clear about what was required of them in their jobs (i.e. high role clarity), and employees reported that they were rarely asked to do things that conflicted with their own personal judgement, or with others' expectations (low role conflict).

However, the research showed that levels of autonomy and decision-making influence were low compared to other companies. For example, decisions were made about aspects such as new equipment and changes to procedures without the input of the shop floor. Also, levels of autonomy over work methods and timing (e.g., when to start and finish things) were low. For example, only 40% of production employees had high scores for the item 'can you control the methods to use in carrying out your work?'. The percentage of high scorers in other manufacturing companies surveyed around the same time ranged from 32 to 73 (median of 68). Jobs were also fairly narrow (e.g. only 41% had high scores for the questionnaire item 'do you do a range of different things') and opportunities for learning were very low (only 13% had high scores on the item 'do you get the opportunity to develop new skills'). The evidence thus suggested routine jobs in which employees had little challenge and influence.

In terms of well-being, the picture was more positive. Levels of general stress were mostly low. Only 14% had more than two symptoms of psychological strain (assessed using the General Health Questionnaire), whereas the range for other companies recently surveyed by the researchers was 14 to 40% (median of 21%). Levels of commitment to the company were extremely high. 80% were 'proud to tell people which company they worked for', which compares favourably to other companies' scores.

Generally, the workforce was one in which a highly committed workforce with good levels of well-being were working in rather routine and unchallenging jobs that did not afford them much autonomy. The organisation needed to make better use of the talents of its workforce.

8.4 WHAT THE COMPANY DID: AN EARLY FORM OF LEAN PRODUCTION TEAMS

The company introduced what they called a 'cell certification team initiative' to improve production processes. The cell certification process was introduced to replace an earlier total quality initiative involving continuous improvement teams. The new management team introduced after the company was bought out felt that the continuous improvement teams had lost impetus, and also that they did not involve the whole team. In contrast, the teams formed as part of the cell certification process involved all team members and focused on day-to-day tasks. A team leader was responsible for managing team activities. Most often, the team leader was also the traditional supervisor. There were no structural changes associated with the implementation of these teams, and teams continued to be managed by supervisors who directed and controlled their activities.

The cell certification process was as follows. First a 'cell', or team, was formed involving a group of assemblers who needed to work together to complete their tasks. After the team had been formed, the team members engaged in a series of activities to simplify the production process. This involved making production uncertainties visible and then systematically removing these uncertainties by simplifying and standardising the production process. Team activities included:

- identifying customer needs
- flowcharting processes
- identifying inputs and outputs to the team
- identifying risks
- developing understanding of processes, suppliers, and customers
- measuring critical parameters
- removing wasteful activities.

Efforts were made to simplify and standardise technical procedures (e.g. the flow of parts through the team) as well as work group-work procedures such as developing training, health and safety plans. A team was 'certified' when all of the processes had been measured and standardised, or were 'in control'. Essentially, the teams represented an early stage in the implementation of lean production because they focused heavily on employees simplifying the procedures (removing 'wasted effort') and then standardising how they were performed.

Teams were taking an average of 18 months to reach the point where they were 'certified'. Some pilot teams had been introduced before the start of the study, and were given extensive support from management. These teams were highly successful, which led management to introduce the lean teams more broadly throughout production.

8.5 IMPACT OF CHANGE: WHAT EFFECT DID LEAN TEAMS HAVE ON ASSEMBLERS AND THEIR JOBS?

The first important set of questions concerns the effect of lean teams on jobs, addressing such question as: how were jobs affected by the introduction of lean teams? Were levels of stress reduced and was job satisfaction enhanced?

The survey information was analysed to see what changes, if any, occurred as a result of the introduction of lean teams. Change over time was compared for two groups:

- people who moved into lean teams (N = 75).
- people who remained in traditional work group (N = 235)

  (Note that employees working in moving lines were excluded from these analyses).

The results can be summarized as follows: **Lean teams had little impact on the quality of people's jobs and little impact on people's well-being** (*see* Appendix A for tables showing the detailed figures). In fact, there was a decrease in the amount of autonomy employees' have over their work methods, and a decrease in job variety, for those in lean teams. However, these aspects *also decreased* for the traditional work groups, suggesting the negative job effects were due to site-wide lean production changes rather than particularly due to the effect of lean 'teams' per se. One site-wide change that might have lowered method control and job variety was the simplification of procedures that arose from designing products for 'manufacturability' (i.e. product designs that are easy to manufacture). Another potential explanation was the introduction of the Technical Resources department, which was a department created specifically to simplify work procedures.

Levels of job-related anxiety, job-related depression, and intrinsic satisfaction did not change for those in lean teams. However, these aspects did decline slightly for those in traditional work groups, suggesting that being in teams might have had some compensatory effect.

What can be concluded from these findings? One conclusion is that introducing an early form of lean teams had little or no effect on job quality and employee well-being. However, another possibility is that some lean teams had positive effects whilst some had negative effects, **resulting in no overall average change**. Evidence from retrospective questions asked after the introduction of lean teams supported this interpretation. Retrospective questions, in which employees were asked to reflect back and think about how teams affected them, showed that some people felt the quality of their jobs had improved (36%), most felt the quality of their jobs had remained the same (59%), and only a few felt their jobs were worse as a result of the lean teams (5%). The researchers therefore conducted additional analyses to identify why people differed in their responses to teams.

8.6 WHAT IS THE EFFECT OF TEAMS THAT VARY IN THEIR DESIGN QUALITY?

Interviews with team members suggested that the lean teams varied on two important dimensions. The first was the degree of **participation in team activities**. Some team members, for example, reported having no input into important decisions and not being encouraged to contribute in team meetings. They felt that the teams were dominated by one or two individuals, such as an engineer or a team leader, and that they had little influence over what happened.

A second important dimension was **support for team activities.** In some cases, team members felt their team activities were not supported by their immediate supervisor or manager. For example, some supervisors did not allow team members sufficient time for team activities, and did not encourage employees to undertake the activities. Likewise, in some cases there was a lack of support from other departments whose co-operation was needed to carry out the cell certification process successful. For example, the purchasing department needed to respond to requests to purchase new equipment within a reasonable time scale, and the engineering department needed to respond to requests for changes to product design or the design of procedures in order to progress satisfactorily. If these support departments were not responsive, this meant team members' suggestions could not be acted upon.

The researchers measured these important aspects of team functioning in the follow-up questionnaire. They then repeated the above analyses looking at change over time separately for four types of lean teams. The four categories were:

- Lean Team Type 1: Low participation and low support (N = 31).
- Lean Team Type 2: High participation but low support (N = 17).
- Lean Team Type 3: High support but low participation (N = 17)
- Lean Team Type 4: High participation and high support (N = 39)

Each group was examined separately to see how their jobs and well-being changed with the introduction of lean teams. The results showed that Lean Team Type 1 (i.e., people in teams where they had little involvement and low support) experienced negative consequences for their jobs and well-being. They had reduced autonomy over the timing and methods of their work, they reported using fewer skills, and they had less general participation in decision-making. They were much less satisfied with their job quality, and their levels of depression at work increased significantly. There was no substantive positive or negative change for the other groups.

Figure 1 shows the relative changes for the 4 groups for job satisfaction. This figure shows how job satisfaction declined a great deal for those in poor quality lean teams (Lean Team Type 1), but there was no substantive decline in job satisfaction for the other groups.

The figure also shows that the teams differ in their level of job satisfaction at Time 2 but they are much more clustered together at time 1 (statistical analyses show the group differences are statistically significant at Time 2 but not at Time 1). This means that the employees started off with similar levels of job satisfaction, but after the introduction of lean teams, they had different levels of job satisfaction according to the quality of their team. As the figure shows, the team with the highest job satisfaction is where employees are in high participation/ high support teams, and lowest where the teams lack both participation and support. These results are consistent with the investigations of change over time, and show that lean teams have a negative effect on well-being when participation and support for teams are low.

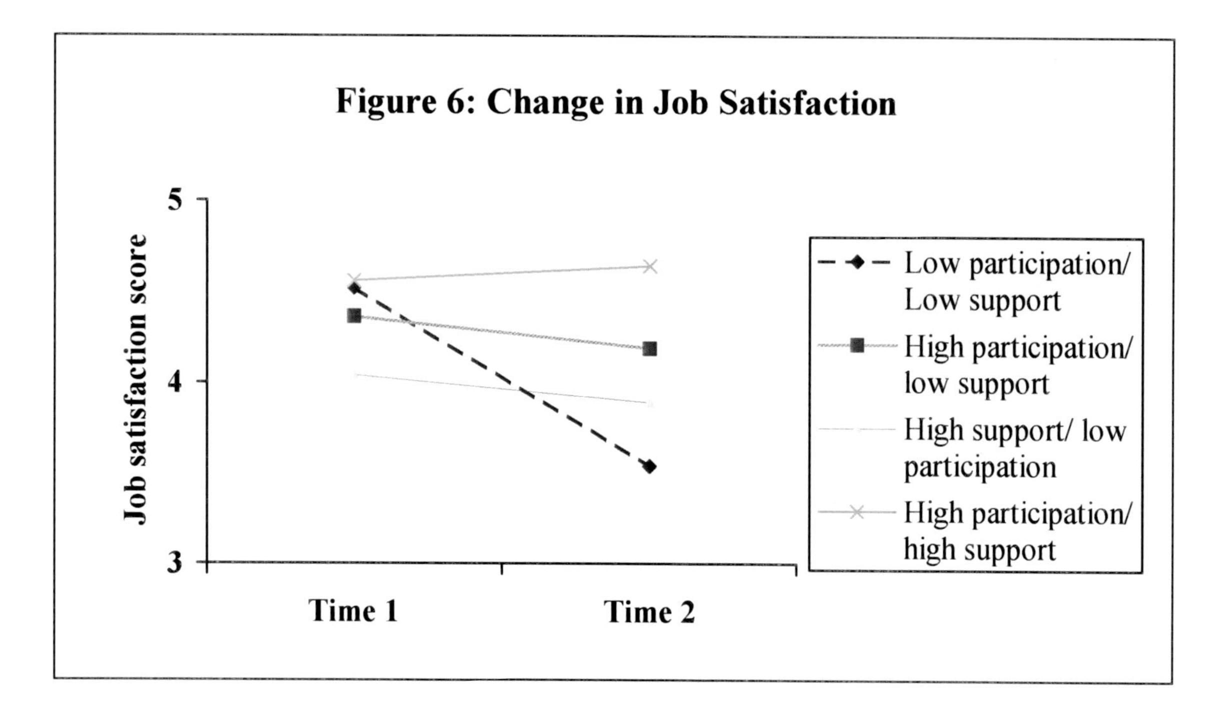

Figure 6: Change in Job Satisfaction

Figure 2 shows the same set of results for job-related depression. Job-related depression increased for those in poor quality teams in which people were uninvolved and unsupported, but depression levels remained about the same for those who moved into better quality teams. Figure 2 also shows how people started off with similar levels of job-related depression, but that after the introduction of lean teams, depression was significantly higher amongst those in poor quality teams.

The message from the results so far is: when implementing lean production style teams, it is important (a) to ensure employees have an opportunity to participate in on-going team decisions and to make suggestions, and (b) for managers and support staff to actively support and be responsive to team activities. Introducing lean teams and then not allowing employees to participate in relevant decisions, or failing to support the teams, is likely to be damaging to people's well-being at work.

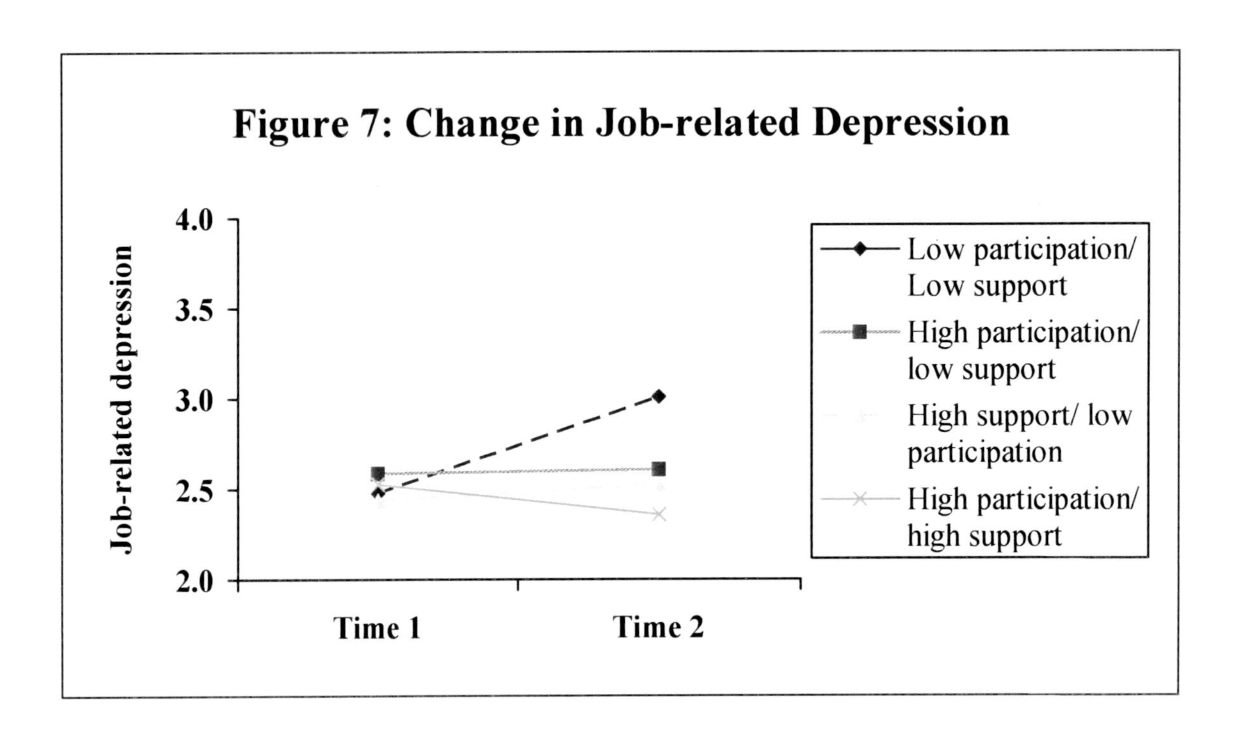

8.7 EFFECT OF LEAN TEAMS ON PERFORMANCE

What about the effects of lean teams on performance? The general view of management was that lean teams had been successful in aspects such as reducing waste and improving quality. The researchers asked employees for their views about this issue. Responses were mixed. In terms of efficiency, only a few people (5%) felt that efficiency got worse, nearly half thought there had been no impact (49%) and over one third (40%) felt efficiency had improved as a result of the teams. Employees were more positive about the quality benefits. Only 4% felt that quality had gotten worse as a result of teams, 37% felt quality had stayed much the same, and 60% felt quality had improved. Additional analyses showed that, as with the effects on jobs and well-being, those employees who believed that there were performance benefits, belonged to particular types of teams. Analyses showed that the highest-performing teams were:

- **High participation** teams in which employees had input into felt encouraged to contribute to team meetings and had a stake in important decisions.
- **High support** teams in which there was active support for team activities, especially from the team leader.

These were by far the strongest aspects of teams that were important for efficiency and quality. In addition, although to a lesser degree, employees in teams that had been together a longer time and were closer to being certified were also likely to report the greatest performance benefits. **These findings suggest that, not only will there be benefits for employee well-being, there**

will be performance benefits if teams are designed to be participative and if they are actively supported.

8.8 WHAT FACTORS WILL HELP PROMOTE PARTICIPATION WITHIN LEAN TEAMS AND SUPPORT FOR LEAN TEAMS?

Some additional investigation by the researchers revealed some potential important facilitators of good teams. First, **employees in smaller teams reported more participation**. This suggests that as teams get too large (e.g. some of the teams in this company had more than 20 employees) then it will be harder to encourage participation amongst all employees. Small teams should be designed to encourage greater employee participation.

Second, **workload** was negatively associated employees' feeling of support for their team. This suggests that teams with a high work load feel the most dissatisfied with the support they receive. Perhaps this is because busy teams who are then expected to do team activities on top of their every day work are likely to *need* extra support. The implication to draw from this is that particular priority should be given to supporting very busy teams when implementing lean teams.

Third, a **coaching-oriented supervisory style** was positively associated with both participation and support within lean teams. A coaching supervisory style is one in which the supervisor actively engages in the following sorts of behaviours:

- lets group members know how to improve their performance
- encourages people to work for her/ him as a team
- provides, or arranges for, help that the group needs to work effectively
- encourages people who work for him/ her to exchange opinions and ideas
- co-ordinates the group's activities to achieve maximum performance

Unlike self-managing teams, the lean teams implemented within the company were introduced without any structural change; that is, team members continued to report to a supervisor. The leadership qualities of this person are therefore crucial. The supervisor needs to be able to coach and encourage employees, help them to obtain the resources and support they need, delegate, resolve conflicts within the team, set goals, and motivate continued effort in the face of set-backs. Within Company Trucker, many of the supervisors were traditional 'foremen'. Most had no training in a more coaching-oriented style of leadership, and many believed good supervision to mean closely directing and controlling employee activities. Yet, **results of this study suggest that the most effective supervision style is a coaching-oriented one.**

8.9 SUMMARY

On the whole, there was a small positive benefit of implementing the early form of lean teams for employees and their jobs, but this benefit was not large. At the best, team working seem to have protected employees from some of the negative effects of wider-scale lean production changes being implemented in the company. These benefits were only obtained when there was high participation within the team as well as a great deal of active support for the team from supervisors, managements and support departments. Indeed, in lean teams where participation and support were both low, employees became more depressed and dissatisfied with their jobs. The research also suggested that lean teams with high participation and support are also the most likely to increase efficiency and quality.

Factors associated with more team participation were having a smaller team and an effective supervisor. Teams most likely to be happy with the support they received were those with supervisors who have a coaching-oriented style and those with a lower work load.

It is important to note that the lean teams reported in this company were in the **early stages of lean production teams**. It is possible that fully-fledged lean production teams, involving the removal of all buffers between stages of the production process followed by extreme levels of process simplification and standardisation, will have more severe negative effects on job quality and employee mental health.

8.10 LESSONS LEARNED

Simply forming teams is no guarantee of success. Telling employees they are a team and then expecting them to sort everything out for themselves will lead to benefits in some (exceptional) cases, no change in most cases, and negative outcomes in others. This study results in the following recommendations for those planning to implement any type of lean production team.

- Design teams so that they will be participative. The teams should be structured in such a way that employees can contribute to decision-making and so that they are fully involved in team activities. The importance of employee involvement is particularly acute in lean teams because part of the process involves standardising procedures. If employees have to follow standard procedures, yet lack any opportunity to develop or change these standard procedures, the lack of control over procedures is likely to be stressful.

- Ensure team leaders and/or supervisors have the necessary skills to support teams and facilitate participative decision-making. Supervisors might be used to more directive and controlling styles of supervision, but a coaching-oriented style is likely to be more effective for managing teams. It is likely that those who have been traditional supervisors will need training and development to make the transition to team working.
- Ensure that the teams' activities are actively supported by supervisors, managers, and support departments. If team members go beyond the call of duty to come up with ideas for improving their work area, and then are faced with resistance or in-action from those who should support them, the team members will soon become demotivated.
- Prioritise support for busy teams. If teams are already busy and under pressure, then it is even more important to support them if it is expected that they take on additional duties. Otherwise team working will soon fall by the wayside, and may even be stressful for the individuals involved.
- Design teams that are not too large so that all members have a chance to get involved.

8.11 FURTHER INFORMATION AND READING

An academic version of this study is currently in preparation by S.K. Parker. A case based on the introduction of a moving assembly line within the same organisation is in: Parker, S. K., & Sprigg, C. A., (1998). A move backwards? The introduction of a moving assembly line. In Parker, S. K., Jackson, P. R., Sprigg, C.A., and Whybrow, A.C. (Eds.) *Organizational interventions to reduce the impact of poor work design*. HSE Books: Norwich, UK.

8.12 READINGS ABOUT LEAN PRODUCTION

Jackson, P. R., & Mullarkey, S. (2000). Lean production teams and health in garment manufacture. *Journal of Occupational Health Psychology*, 5, 231-245.

Monden, Y. (1994). *Toyota Production System (2nd Edition)*. New York: Chapman & Hall.

Turnbull, P. J. (1988). The limits to "Japanisation" - Just-in-time, labour relations and the UK automotive industry. *New Technology, Work and Employment*, 3, 7-20.

Womack, J. P., Jones, D. T., & Roos, D. (1990). *The Machine that Changed the World.* New York: Rawson Associates.

APPENDIX FOR STUDY 2

Table 1

	Timing Control			Method Control			Skill Variety		
	T1	T3	F[1]	T1	T3	F[1]	T1	T3	F[1]
Lean teams (n=75)	3.24	3.11	1.41	3.53	3.34	3.34+	3.00	2.66	9.69 *
	(1.02)	(1.05)		(0.79)	(0.78)		(0.89)	(0.86)	
Traditional groups [3] (n=238)	3.27	3.26	<1	3.51	3.34	6.60*	3.14	2.78	27.17 ***
	(1.00)	(1.04)		(0.78)	(0.87)		(0.83)	(0.99)	
F[2]	<1	6.75*		<1	2.92*		<1	1.56	

[1] Statistical test for change over time (an asterixed value shows a statistically significant change, the more asterixes the larger the change)

[2] Statistical test for differences across group at each time period (an asterixed value shows a statistically significant difference, the more asterixes the larger the difference)

[3] This group excludes any employees who were in a moving line (they are analysed separately)

Table 2

	Job-related Anxiety			Job-related Depression			Intrinsic Job Satisfaction		
	T1	T3	F[1]	T1	T3	F[1]	T1	T3	F[1]
Lean teams (n=75)	2.33	2.34	<1	2.44	2.55	<1	4.39	4.22	1.15
	(0.72)	(0.76)		(0.69)	(0.77)		(0.97)	(1.01)	
Traditional groups [3] (n=238)	2.41	2.45	<1	2.40	2.59	3.88*	4.54	4.16	15.38 ***
	(0.63)	(0.62)		(0.61)	(0.64)		(0.84)	(1.00)	
F[2]	<1	1.98		<1	4.05*		<1	3.94**	

[1] Statistical test for change over time (an asterixed value shows a statistically significant change, the more asterixes the larger the change)

[2] Statistical test for differences across group at each time period (an asterixed value shows a statistically significant difference, the more asterixes the larger the difference)

[3] This group excludes any employees who were in a moving line (they are analysed separately)

9. STUDY 3
THE TRANSITION BETWEEN TRADITIONAL TEAM WORKING AND SELF-MANAGED TEAM WORKING

9.1 SUMMARY

This study focuses on the implementation of self-managed teams. Researchers surveyed production teams two years after they had undergone the transition from traditional work teams to self-managed team working. This transition had relative degrees of success. Whilst some teams had become self-managing, other teams had made little progress in the move away from traditional team working. The results from this study suggest that self-management increases both employee well-being and team effectiveness. Self-management also increased employees' proactivity by increasing their self-confidence to carry out a broader range of tasks. However, the full benefits of self-managed team working were only achieved if all team members rather than a select few within the team became more self-managing.

9.2 THE SETTING

This study reports on the implementation of self-managed team working in a chemical processing plant based in the UK. As part of a plan to move towards a flatter, less hierarchical structure the company decided to move from traditional (supervisor-led) team working to a self-managed form of team working. Self-managing teams were implemented in the production workforce two years prior to our study. However, despite a very structured and planned implementation strategy, the initiative was more successful for some teams than others. This study therefore enabled us the opportunity to compare self-managed team working to more traditional team working within a sample of teams that conducted similar tasks within the same company.

9.3 BEFORE THE IMPLEMENTATION OF SELF-MANAGED TEAMS

Prior to self-managed team working each team had a supervisor who worked on their shift in an office close to where the team worked. This supervisor directed and organised the teams' work on a shift to shift basis and was not responsible for any other teams. Under this organisational system the team members therefore carried out the core tasks whilst the supervisors managed the process (e.g., planning, manning, quality control) and made the major decisions.

However, the company decided that it wanted to move towards a flatter, less hierarchical structure with the aim of removing barriers to development and creating a system that was easier to both understand and work in. Self-managing teams were implemented as a way of achieving this since they entailed the teams taking on management tasks in addition to the core tasks of their job. In addition the supervisor post was removed, thus creating the desired flatter organisational structure, and a team leader was appointed within each team so as to provide a focal point in the team.

9.4 DESCRIPTION OF THE IMPLEMENTATION OF SELF-MANAGED TEAMS

The change management team specified the roles and responsibilities of both the team leaders and the team members. This information was clearly and efficiently communicated to all personnel on site. The company recognised the fact that the implementation of self-managed team working is an 'evolutionary processes', and therefore decided to gradually increase the responsibilities of the teams in phases.

9.4.1 Phase 1: Appointment of the team leader

Within each team, a team leader was appointed by managers.

9.4.2 Phase 2: 'Training and Planning' stage

This phase involved teams having training in the principles of self-managing teams (e.g., definitions and descriptions of the key concepts, examples of the type of activities it would involve). In addition, within each area, managers (in combination with the teams) developed definitions of the role and responsibilities of both the team members and the team leaders.

9.4.3 Phase 3: 'Start-up' stage

This phase involved the team taking on key initial responsibilities of planning and co-ordination, procedures, shift hand-over, appraisal, cover arrangements, and resolution of conflict within the team.

9.4.4 Phase 4: Developing team responsibilities

At this stage the teams took on more key responsibilities such as; training and coaching within the team, night order book responsibilities, health and safety activities, optimisation of the plant including key performance indicators, and plant development.

9.4.5 Phase 5: Additional responsibilities

This last stage involved the team taking over the final responsibilities of the supervisor. This included taking responsibility for emergency response co-ordination, training and assessment, team budget control and group optimisation. At this stage in the implementation process, the supervisor role was removed totally. Some of the supervisors took early retirement whereas others took jobs else where in the company.

Although this implementation process took place across the whole site it was achieved with relative degrees of success. Two years after the implementation of self managing teams, which was when the evaluation (i.e. surveys, management ratings, etc) was conducted, there were some teams that took on all the self-managing team responsibilities and other teams where the management team in their area had to pick up the supervisors' responsibilities when the supervisors were taken off shift.

9.5 THE BENEFICIAL EFFECT OF SELF-MANAGED TEAM WORKING

To ascertain how beneficial self-managed team working was, the first step was to identify how self-managing the teams were. The best measure of self-managed team working is the degree to which teams were conducting various self-managed tasks (e.g. ordering their own supplies, allocating jobs). However there was no need for all team members to be involved in <u>all</u> of these tasks (i.e., complete multiskilling), since what was critical was that, as a team, the tasks were being carried out. Self-management was therefore calculated at the team level as **the degree to which at least one person in the team was conducting a list of self-managed activities** (assessed via survey).

It was found that teams that were more self-managing were rated by managers as performing better, displaying more initiative and innovation, and exhibiting more organisational citizenship behaviours (i.e. behaviours that are not a required part of the job but which contribute to the effectiveness of the organisation) than those teams that were not self-managing (see figure 1). This suggests that where teams have become self-managing, there are organisational benefits. This is further illustrated by several comments made by team members. For example, one team member said *"I agree that self-managing teams are the way forward in improving work standards and relations between colleagues".*

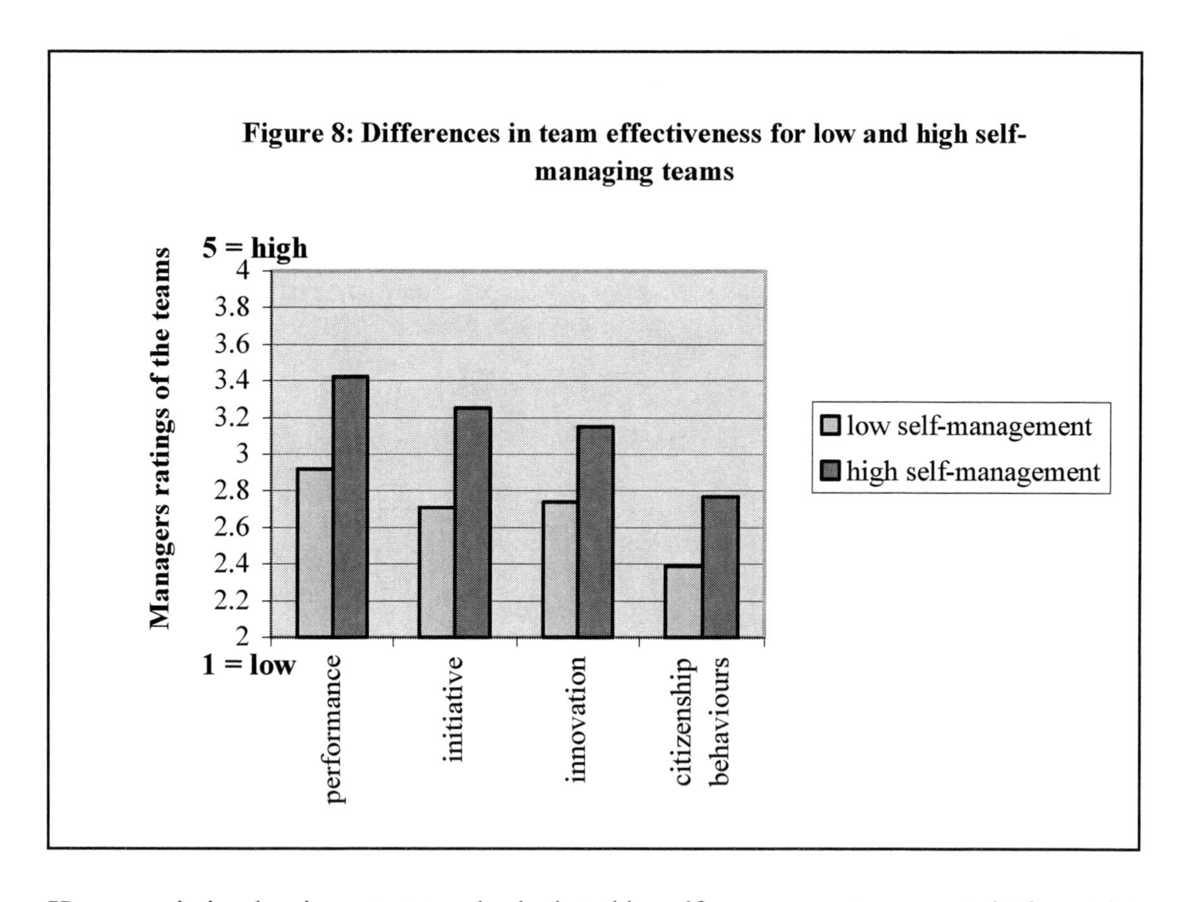

Figure 8: Differences in team effectiveness for low and high self-managing teams

However, it is also important to check that this self-management was not detrimental to employee well-being. In analyses comparing those individuals with high self-management from those with low self-management, the researchers found some interesting differences. In terms of work characteristics, researchers found those team members who were highly self-managing reported having greater autonomy about how and when to do tasks and had greater clarity about what their role involved, but a higher workload than those individuals who were not very self-managing (*see* Figure 2). Interestingly there was no significant difference in the role conflict reported by these two groups of employees, that is, neither group suffered from having conflicting role expectations. In general, self-management therefore had a positive effect on work design, especially since the workload exhibited by the highly self-managing individuals, although higher, was not excessive since it was on a par with the level of work load reported in other companies that we have recently surveyed.

The different effects on work design suggest that self-managing teams might have a mixed effect on employee mental health. Analyses of the data from the survey confirmed findings reported in past research. That is, better mental health (assessed by looking at employee stress, job satisfaction and organisational commitment) was associated with high autonomy, high role clarity, low role conflict and low workload.

In terms of employee mental health outcomes there were differences between those teams who were highly self-managing and those who had little self-management (*see* Figure 3). In particular it was found that employees in high self-managing teams were more satisfied in their job, more committed to the organisation, more secure about the future, but felt more stress at work. The greater work-related stress in high self managing teams is probably attributable to the higher work load in these teams, which is evidenced by several comments from team members. For example, one technician commented *"every week more and more work is being delegated down to technicians. Stress levels are rising because of this. When will it stop?"*.

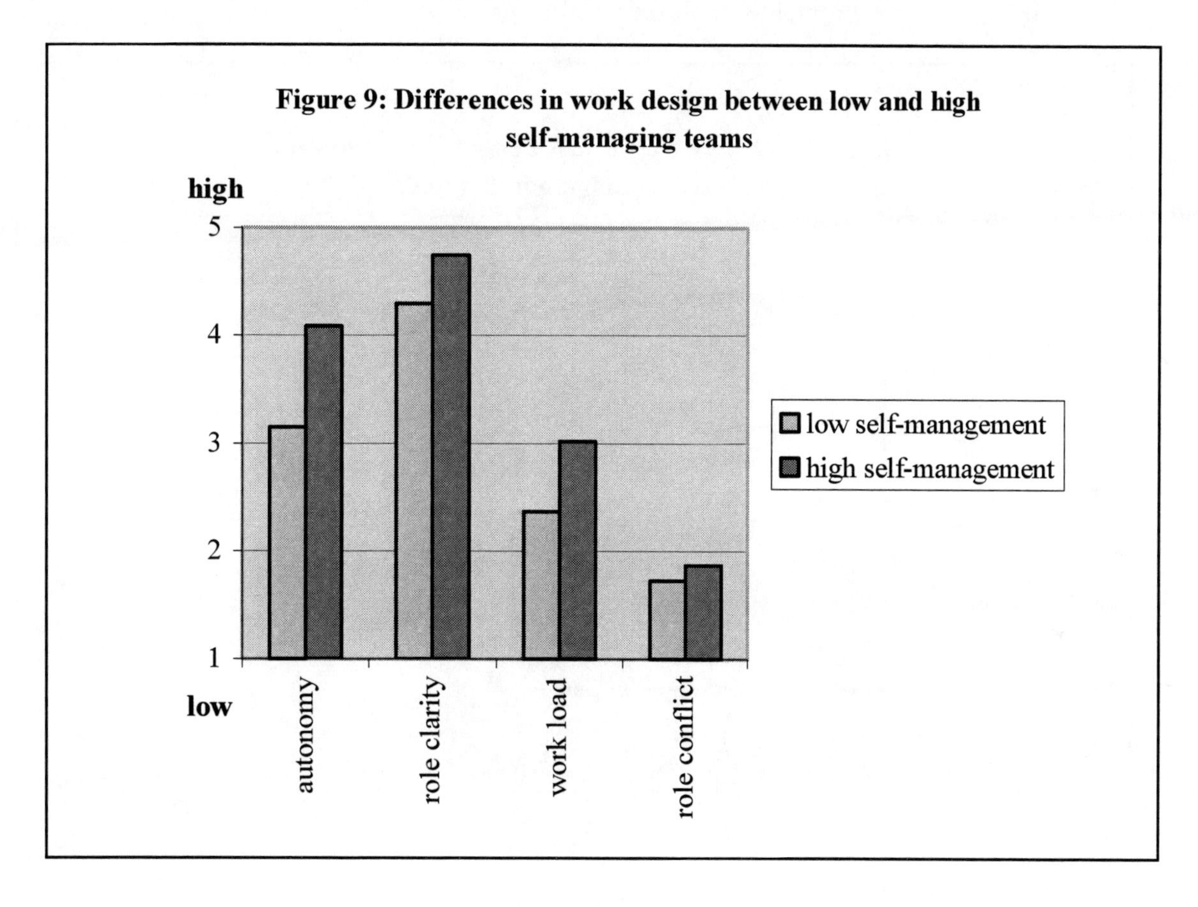

Figure 9: Differences in work design between low and high self-managing teams

In terms of employee mental health outcomes there were differences between those teams who were highly self-managing and those who had little self-management (*see* Figure 3). In particular it was found that employees in high self-managing teams were more satisfied in their job, more committed to the organisation, more secure about the future, but felt more stress at work. The greater work-related stress in high self managing teams is probably attributable to the higher work load in these teams, which is evidenced by several comments from team members. For example, one technician commented *"every week more and more work is being delegated down to technicians. Stress levels are rising because of this. When will it stop?"*.

Within this company we find that the levels of stress in the high self-managing group were not so excessive as to be concerning since they were lower than UK norms for production employees (high self-managing teams = 3.36; low self-managing teams = 3.09; UK production norm = 3.42 - *see* Mullarkey *et al.*, 1999). Therefore, because it was linked to higher job satisfaction, one could conclude that, overall, self-management was beneficial to employee well-being within this company. However, the increased levels of stress within self-managed teams does suggest that organisations need to be aware that implementing self-managed teams may increase stress levels and it is essential this increased stress is **monitored** to ensure that it is not at a level that is detrimental to employees well-being.

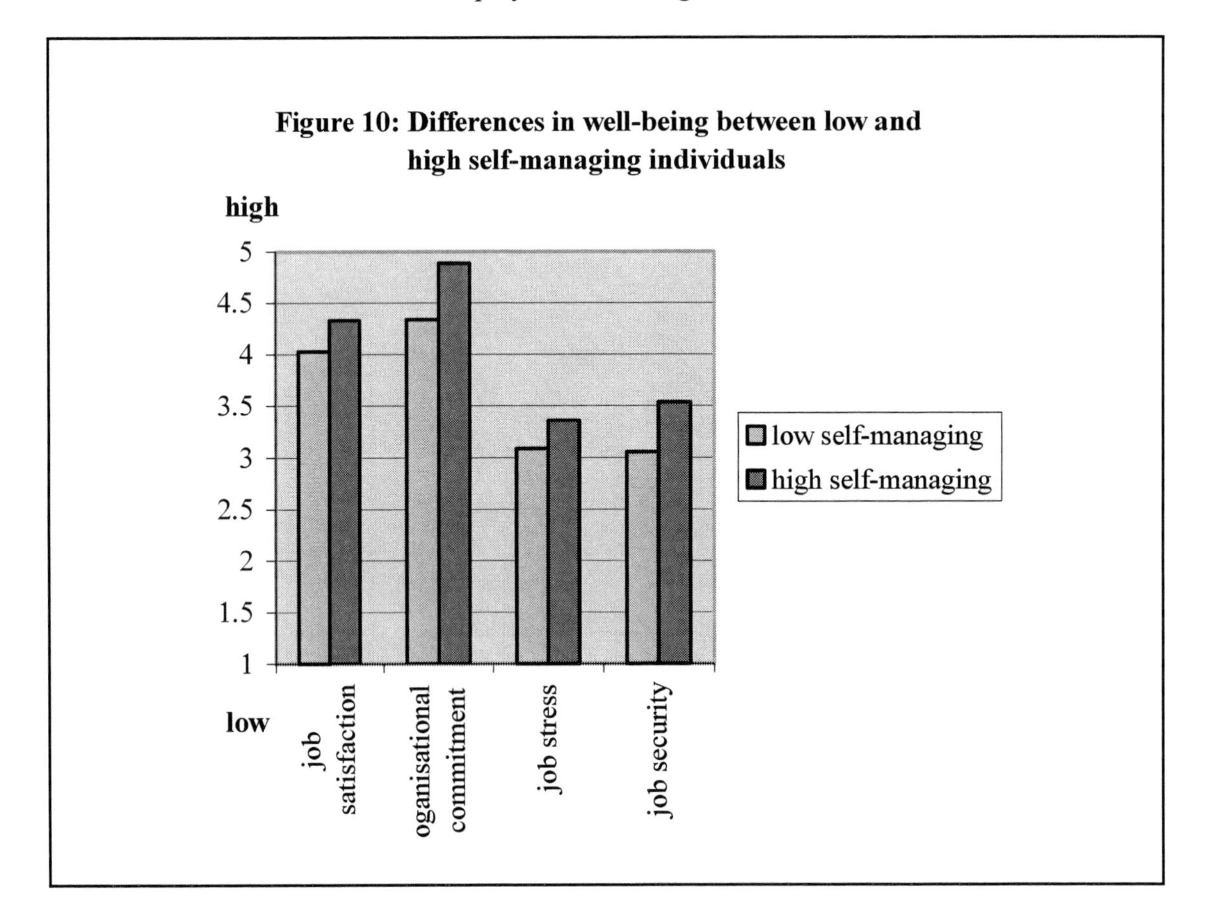

Figure 10: Differences in well-being between low and high self-managing individuals

This comparison between high self-managing and low self-managing teams was also evident from team members' comments. For instance, some team members made very positive comments about the success of self-managing teams:

- *"I feel that self-managing teams have helped my team improve".*
- *"Self-managing teams have in my opinion improved greatly the way we work"*
- *"It provides an opportunity for all to be heard and have a say in what and how we work as a team. Gives support to the weaker members who may be quiet, but have skills and knowledge where with encouragement will share with others"*

Whereas others had very negative perceptions of self managing teams: for example:

- *"We may be called self managing teams but we will always be directed by manufacturing managers"*
- *"Self managing teams do not work because of human behaviour"*

9.6 CHARACTERISTICS OF SELF-MANAGED TEAMS

The researchers analysed the data (from both the survey and from interviews) to determine the characteristics of successful self-managed teams.

Successful self-managed teams could be characterised as having:

- **Positive team relations**

  High self-managing teams seemed to have a unity and agreeableness that was lacking in the low self-managed teams. In contrast, the low self-managed teams appeared to have a greater degree of animosity amongst team members. For example, technicians from high self-managing teams made comments such as: *"everyone works with each other"* and *"if there is something gone wrong, everyone will muck in and try to get it sorted"*. In contrast a technician from a low self-managing team summed up the relationships between team members as *"I don't think we are a proper unit as such"*.

- **Flexible and diverse skill mix**

  The results also showed that high self-managing teams had a greater degree of different skills within the team and had more flexibility amongst team members. Further, the members of high self-managed teams appeared to be more motivated to work to the best of their abilities. This is illustrated by the fact that a member of a highly self-managing team said *"I think we all perform to the best of our abilities, and we all use our skills to the best of our abilities"*

- **Broader view of their role**

  It was apparent from the data that low self-managed teams had a more restricted view of their role and were more reluctant to take on responsibility. These teams also had very clear boundaries seeing their role as 'doing what is in the order book'. The low self-managed teams also wanted a team leader who directed and controlled their work like a supervisor, whereas the high self-managed teams, although seeing the importance of having a good team leader, sought advice and coaching rather than direction. Finally, members of low self-managed teams commented that there was no motivation within the team to get better since there was no incentive to becoming an excellent team.

9.7 BARRIERS TO SELF-MANAGED TEAM WORKING

So, how can teams become more self-managing? From our interviews it appears that there are three important barriers to self-managed team working.

- **Management style**

  The most salient way in which management hindered the development of self-managed team working was too much "controlling" supervision. This is illustrated by the multitude of comments we received on this issue. Illustrative comments are:

  - *"We may be called SMTs, but we are always directed by manufacturing managers"*
  - *"SMTs would on the face of it seem to be a good way to go, but management hierarchy tend to dictate the way we are working at the moment"*
  - *"Management will never let you become an SMT and that has been proved"*
  - *"We are only SMTs as long as management agrees"*
  - *"SMTs can work very well provided interference from above is kept at bay"*
  - *"We will never be self-managing as long as the manufacturing team leader dictates his views and insists on doing things his way. It is still a case of them and us"*

  There were also issues surrounding managers changing their priorities (e.g. sometimes focusing on productivity, sometimes focusing on safety, sometimes focusing on team working) and managers not fully understanding what jobs entail.

- **Poor Communication**

  A lack of face-to face meetings between team members and day shift personnel was also seen as a barrier to self-managed team working amongst low self-managed teams. It is likely that such communication helps the development of self-management by providing guidance and support, as well as a greater sense of the "bigger picture".

  The results also suggest that poor communication amongst team members can hinder self-managed team working.

- **Lack of detailed feedback**

  Low self-managing teams found it difficult to see how they could improve because they feel that they are not given an explanation of where they are going "wrong" and consequently they don't know how to improve. Further, when teams make suggestions to improve work processes or practices, they feel that there is little feedback on whether the idea will be taken up, or how it is progressing.

9.8 THE IMPORTANCE OF INCREASING THE SELF-MANAGEMENT OF ALL TEAM MEMBERS

From informal conversations with some of the technicians and managers the researchers were alerted to the fact that team self-management may have only really applied to a few team members, especially team leaders. The comments below illustrate this:

- *"Management still views the team leader as a focal point. They do not treat team members as equal"*
- *"The management treats team leaders like the old foreman and do not allow this team to be self-managing, always channelling their views through the team leader"*
- *"'Self managing' is being replaced by team leader directed"*
- *"Self managing teams do not operate on Plant A. T.1 (team leader) decides what will be done"*

Therefore, whilst the team may have been succeeding in the transformation into self-managed teams, this may have been solely due to one or two team members taking over the supervisor's role. This is concerning because it implies that some team members may not have been benefiting from the self-managed team working, and that the benefits of self managing teams might be under-realised. To investigate whether or not this was the case, the researchers investigated the effect of self-management (i.e. high self-management vs. low self-management) in teams where team members had either similar or non-similar degrees of self-managed behaviours (i.e. similar vs. non-similar individual level self-management). This gives a 4-cell taxonomy of self-management.

	Team members having similar levels of self-management	**Team members having different levels of self-management**
Low team self-management	Low self-management across all team members	Low self-management as a whole, but with some individuals with high self-management
High team self-management	High self-management across all team members	High self-management but self-management restricted to a few key individuals

Analyses comparing employees' commitment to working at the organisation (organisational commitment) and the job satisfaction of individuals in these different types of teams showed some interesting results. First, in terms of organisational commitment, it was found that there was no difference in commitment based on whether or not team members had a similar degree of self-management. The significant differences only occurred between low and high self-managing teams (with individuals from self-managing teams reporting higher commitment to the organisation) (*see* Figure 4). In other words, it did not matter whether or not *all* team members were self-managing, so long as the team as a whole was self-managing.

Figure 11: Comparison between types of team on organisational commitment

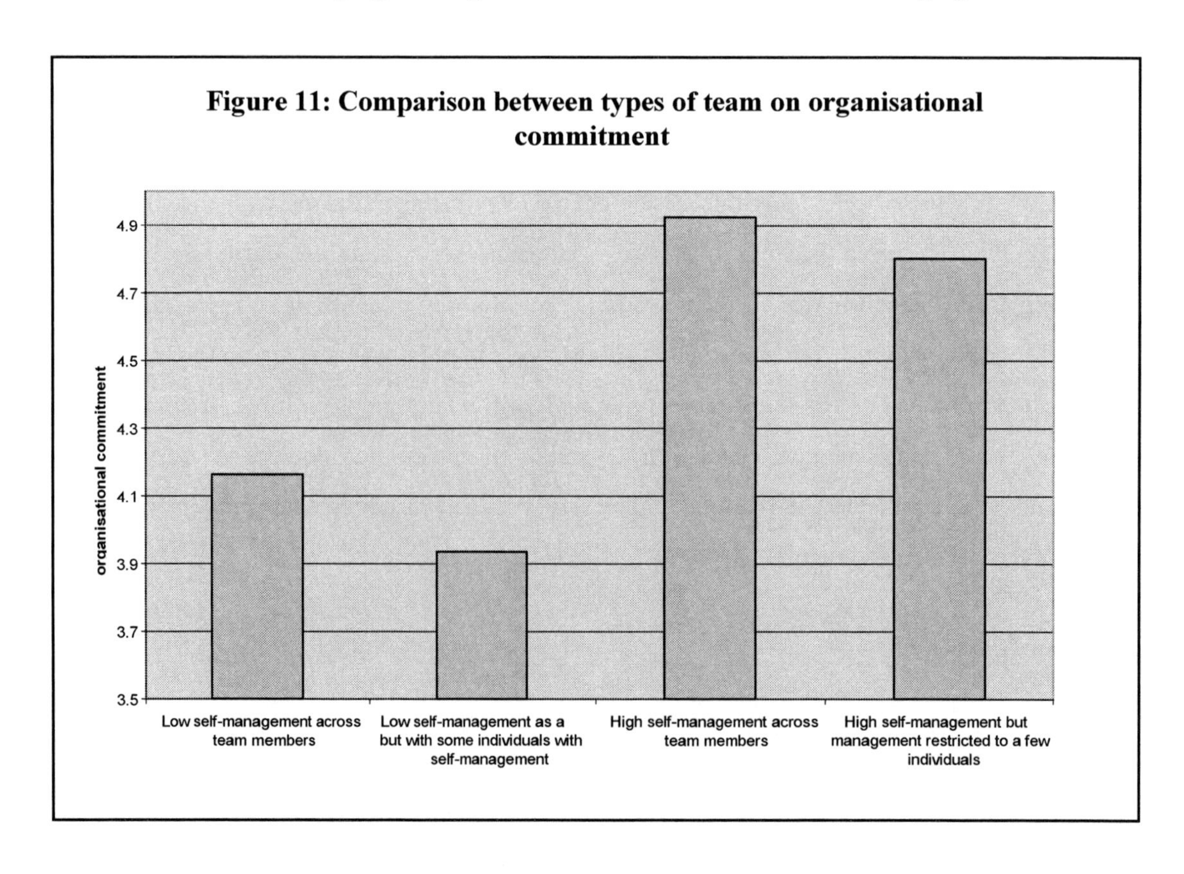

However, in terms of job satisfaction the degree to which all team members were self-managing was found to be important. As can be seen from Figure 5, the benefits of self-managed team working were only felt by those individuals who were in teams where *all* team members were taking on self-managed tasks. Teams where the high self-management of the team was only due to a few team members taking on self-managed responsibilities were not found to differ in their job satisfaction from those individuals in low self-managed teams. These findings suggest that the full job satisfaction benefits of implementing self-managed teams can not be gained unless all team members are encouraged and trained to become more self-managing.

Figure 12: Comparison between types of team on job satisfaction

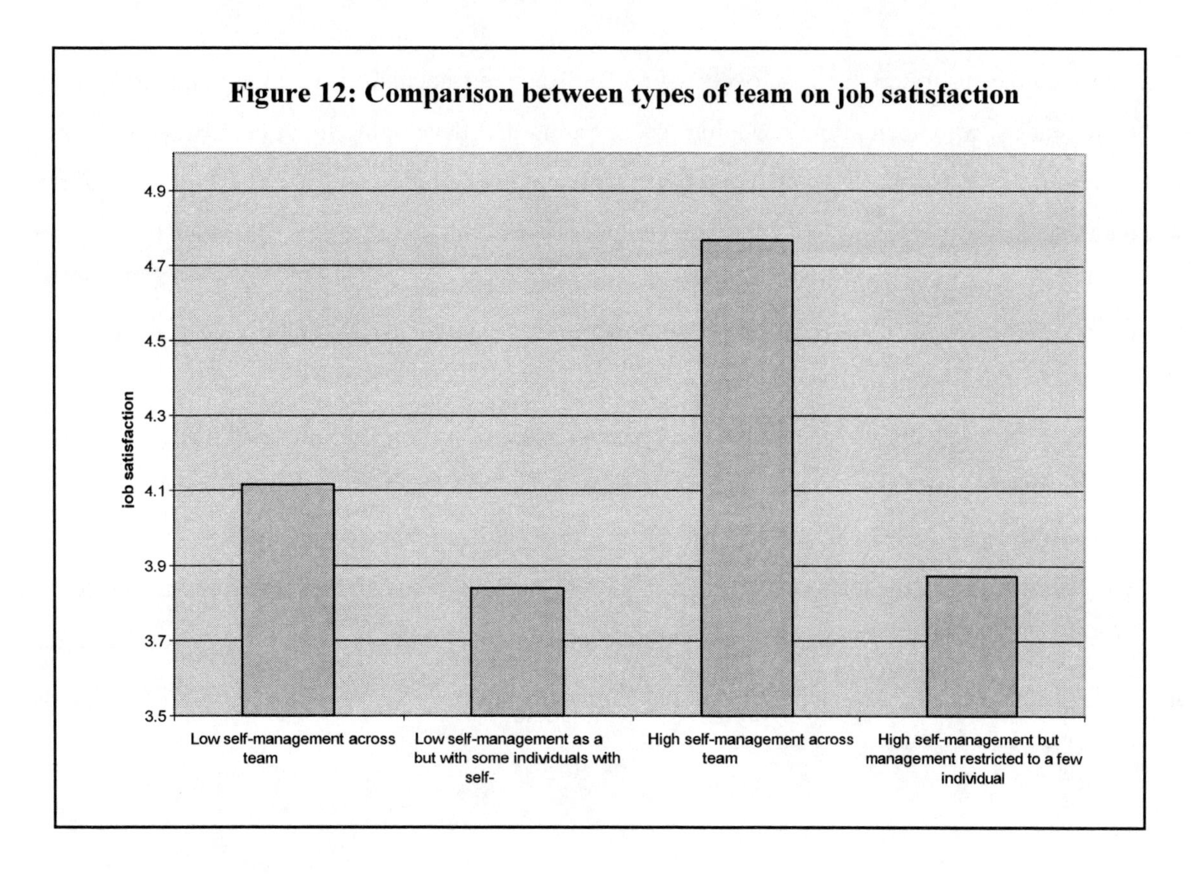

9.9 INCREASING EMPLOYEE INITIATIVE: EMPLOYEE CONFIDENCE AND EFFECTIVE LEADERSHIP

A key element of self-managed team working is that organisations want employees to use their own initiative. As one manager we worked with said, "we want to utilise the brain power we have on the shop floor". The analyses reported earlier suggest that teams that were more self-managed displayed more initiative. The researchers were therefore interested to investigate why and how self-management had this effect. Analyses showed that the link between team autonomy (one aspect of self-management) was positively associated with individual level proactivity. That is, increases in team autonomy were associated with increased proactive behaviour. It would seem likely that this effect arises in part because team autonomy creates the opportunity for team members to be proactive. When employees have little discretion over how and when to do tasks their behaviour will be restricted and therefore they will have little opportunity to use their initiative. Low autonomy can also de-motivate team members' (e.g. Hackman & Oldham, 1980), thus employees may be less likely to try and think of ways of improving things. Our analyses (see appendix for tables of results) however also found that the effect of autonomy on employee proactivity occurs partly because high autonomy promotes team members' confidence in carrying out tasks that go beyond their role, and this confidence encourages team members' to be proactive.

Further analyses found that employees who had effective leadership from their team leader (e.g. team leaders who spend time coaching, encouraging and developing team members) were also more proactive. Leadership was found to promote employees' proactivity in two key ways. First, team leaders were found to encourage proactivity amongst team members most when team autonomy was low. This suggests that, in situations where it is not possible to enhance team members' autonomy, team leaders can still motivate and inspire team members to be proactive.

Second, team leaders can increase team member proactivity through increasing the autonomy that team members have. This seems logical since if managers devolve decision-making responsibility to the teams the team leader can either act in a fairly controlling way (by acting as a supervisor within the team) or the team member can encourage team members to take on some of the responsibility. This final finding therefore reiterates the findings of the previous section, which concluded that the beneficial effects of self-managed team working are greatest when all team members become more self-managing.

9.10 SUMMARY

The results of this case therefore show that: the more self-managing the team (i.e. the more team members have the discretion to make decisions about daily operations), then the better the well-being of team members and the more effective the teams. However, it can be that only one or two team members take on this self-management and do not relinquish any responsibility of self-management to the teams as a whole. In order for the maximum benefits of self-managed team working to be gained **all** team members need to be encouraged and trained to take on self-management responsibilities.

This case also shows that successful self-managing teams can be characterised as having positive team relations, a flexible and diverse skill mix, and a broader view of their role.

Further, in this case, we identified three key barriers to the development of self-managing teams: a "controlling" management style, poor communication and a lack of detailed feedback.

9.11 LESSONS LEARNED

The key implication of this study is that self-managed team working is most beneficial when all or most team members take on self-managing responsibilities. It is not enough to just ensure that the 'team' is self-managing, with in reality either only a few team members taking on all management responsibilities or the team leader acting as a supervisor to the team.

There are many possible ways that self management can be spread throughout the team. For example, the team leader role can be rotated, or teams can have regular development sessions in which all team members are involved in how to progress their team. All team members will need training to support the development of a fully self-managing team.

Further, this case suggests three key recommendations for those who are planning to implement self-managed teams:

- Ensure that managers take a participative or coaching-oriented style. A controlling or directive style of management can hinder SMTs because the control and autonomy is not 'handed down' to the team. Training and development may be necessary in order to help managers take on such a management style.
- Ensure that team members have high levels of communication (both in terms of the quality and the quantity of communication) both amongst themselves and with others in the organisation. Training in interpersonal skills might be required to facilitate this communication.
- Provide teams with detailed information so that they can improve their performance. That is, it is important to make sure that teams are not just told that they need to improve their performance, they need to be given information and guidance as to how to improve their performance. Ideally, when teams are established, they should have access to the necessary information to make their own assessments as to how they are performing (e.g. they should have access to information about customer satisfaction, lead times, quality, etc). However, in the early days of team working, teams might need guidance and training in how to best use this information.

APPENDIX FOR STUDY 3

Table 1:
Summary of results for hierarchical regression analysis testing the interaction between team autonomy and transformational leadership (N = 202)

Step and variables entered	1	2	3	4	5
1. Job tenure	.166+	.191 *	.235*	.250**	.155+
Job type	.086	.065	.029	.037	.063
Age	.107	.115	.093	.069	.139+
2. Transformational leadership		.165*	.057	.034	.063
3. Team autonomy			.297**	.306**	.169*
4. Team autonomy x transformational leadership				-.124+	-.099
					.411**
R^2	.078**	.105**	.179**	.193**	.342**
ΔR^2		027*	.074**	.014+	.149**

Note. The displayed coefficients in the five columns are standardised beta weights at each step. + $p < 0.1$, * $p < 0.05$, ** $p < 0.01$.

Table 2:
Summary of results for hierarchical regression analysis testing transformational leadership as predicting team autonomy (N = 202)

Step and variables entered	1	2
1. Job tenure	-.203*	-.147
Job type	.169*	.121
Age	.057	.073
2. Transformational Leadership		.366**
R^2	.028	.158**
ΔR^2		.130 **

Note. The displayed coefficients in the two columns are standardised beta weights at each step. + $p < 0.1$, * $p < 0.05$, ** $p < 0.01$.

Table 3:
Summary of results for hierarchical regression analysis testing the interaction between team autonomy and transformational leadership as predicting RBSE (N = 202)

Step and variables entered	1	2	3	4
1. Job tenure	.167+	.176+	.224*	.232*
Job type	-.018	-.026	-.066	-.062
Age	-.137	-.134	-.158+	-.170*
2. Transformational leadership		.062	-.058	-.069
3. Team autonomy			.328**	.333**
4. Team autonomy x transformational leadership				-.062
R^2	.021	.025	.116**	.119**
ΔR^2		.004	.091**	.004

Note. The displayed coefficients in the two columns are standardised beta weights at each step. + $p < 0.1$, * $p < 0.05$, ** $p < 0.01$.

ACKNOWLEDGEMENTS

We thank Ruth Stacey for data entry: June Staniland, Vicky Welton and Nicky Wheeler for secretarial support; and Kate Charles, Paul Jackson, Christine Sprigg, Nick Turner and Alison Whybrow for their involvement in field research. We are also very grateful to the employees and managers in the organisations we studied for their co-operation and involvement in the research.

REFERENCES

Applebaun, E., & Batt, R. (1994). The New American Workplace. Ithaca, NY: ILR Press.

Argote, L., & McGrath, J. E. (1993). Group process in organizations: continuity and change. In C. L. Cooper & I. T. Robertson (Eds.), International Review of Industrial and Organizational Psychology (pp. 333-389). Chuchecker: Wiley.

Badham, R, Couchman, R. P., & Selden, D. (1996). Winning the socio-technical wager: Change roles and the implementation of self-managing work cells. In R. J. Koubek & W. Karwowski (Eds.), Manufacturing agility and hybrid automation- I. (pp. 339-343). Louisville, IEA Press.

Banker, R. D., Field, J. M., Schroeder, R. G., & Sinha, K. K. (1996). The impact of work teams on manufacturing performance: a longitudinal field study. Academy of Management Journal, 39(4), 867-890.

Barker, J. R. (1993). Tightening the iron cage: Concertive control in self-managing teams. Administrative Science Quarterly, 38, 408-437.

Beekun, R. I. (1989). Assessing the effectiveness of sociotechnical interventions: Antidote or fad? Human Relations, 47, 87-897.

Benders, J., & Van Hootegem, G. (2000). How the Japanese got teams. In S. Procter & F. Mueller (Eds.), Teamworking (pp. 43-59). Basingstoke: Macmillan Press.

Berggren, C. (1991). Von Ford zu Volvo: Automobilherstellung in Schweden. Berlin: Springer.

Campion, M. A., Medsker, G. J., & Higgs, A. C. (1993). Relations between work group characteristics and effectiveness: Implications for designing effective work groups. Personnel Psychology, 46, 821-850.

Campion, M. A., Papper, E. M., & Medsker, G. J. (1996). Relations between work team characteristics and effectiveness. A replication and extension. Personnel Psychology, 49, 429-689.

Cannon-Bowers, J. A., Oser, R., & Flanagan, D. L. (1992). Work teams in industry: A selected review and proposed framework. In R. W. Swezey & E. Salas (Eds.), Teams: their training and performance (pp. 355-378). Norwood, NJ: Ablex Publishing Corporation.

Carter, A. J., & West, M. A. (1999). Sharing the burden – teamwork in health care settings. In R. Payne & J. Firth-Cozens (Eds.). (pp. 191-202). Stress in Health Professionals: Psychological and organisational causes and interventions. Chichester: Wiley.

Cavanaugh, M.A. Boswell, W.R., Roehling, M.V., & Bourdreau, J.W. (2000). An empirical examination of self-reported work stress among U.S. managers. Journal of Applied Psychology, 85(1), 65-74.

Charles, K. (2000). Semi-Autonomous Work Teams: The Effects of Implementation and Team Membership Change. Unpublished PhD Thesis, University of Sheffield.

Clement, R. (1996). Social Psychology and intergroup communication. Journal of Language and Social Psychology, 15(3), 222-229.

Cohen, S. G., & Ledford, G. E. (1994). The effectiveness of self-managing teams: A quasi-experiment. Human Relations, 47, 13-43.

Cohen, S. G., Ledford, J.R., G. E., & Spreitzer, G. M. (1996). A predictive model of self-managing work team effectiveness. Human Relations, 49, 643-676.

Cordery, J. L. (1996). Autonomous work groups and quality circles. In M. A. West (Ed.), Handbook of Work Group Psychology (pp. 225-246). New York: John Wiley.

Cordery, J. L., Mueller, W. S., & Smith, L. M. (1991). Attitudinal and behavioural effects of autonomous group working: A longitudinal field setting. Academy of Management Journal, 34(2), 464-476.

Cordery, J. L., Wright, B. H., & Wall, T. D. (1997). Towards a more comprehensive and integrated approach to work design: Production uncertainty and self-managing work team performance. Paper presented at the 12th annual conference of the Society for Industrial/Organizational Psychology conference, St. Louis, USA.

Cordery, J.L. & Wright (1999). Production uncertainty as a contextual moderator of employee reactions to job design. Journal of Applied Psychology, 84, 3, 456-463.

Cotton, J. L. (1993). Employee involvement: Methods for improving performance and work attitudes. Sage Publications: London.

Cummings, T. G., & Molloy, E. S. (1977). Improving productivity and the quality of working life. New York: Praeger.

Cummings, T., & Srivastva, S. (1977). Management of work: A socio-technical systems approach. Kent: The Comparative Administration Research Institute of Kent State University.

Cummings, T. (1978). Self-regulated work groups: A socio-technical synthesis. Academy of Management Review, 3, 625-634.

Delbridge, R., Lowe, J., & Oliver, N. (2000). Worker autonomy in lean teams: Evidence from the world automotive industry. In S. Procter & F. Mueller (Eds.), Teamworking (pp. 125-142). Basingstoke: Macmilan Press.

Devine, D. J., Clayton, L. D., Philips, J. L., Dunford, B. B., & Melner, S. B. (1999). Teams in organizations – prevalence, characteristics and effectiveness. Small Group Research, 30, 678-711.

Dyer, W. G. (1987). Team building: Issues and alternatives. (2nd Ed.) Reading, MA: Addison-Wesley.

Elmuti, D., & Kathawala, Y. (1999). Self-managed teams, quality of working life and productivity: a field study. Mid American Journal of Business, 12, 19-25.

Emery, F. E., & Trist, E. L. (1960). Socio-technical systems. In C. H. Churchman & M. Verhulst (Eds.), Management science, models and techniques (Vol. 2, pp. 83-97). New York: Pergamon.

Emery, F. L., & Trist, E. L. (1969). Socio-technical systems. In F. L. Emery (Ed.), Systems Thinking. London: Penguin.

Emery, F. E. (1959). Characteristics of Sociotechnical Systems. London: Tavistock Institute of Human Relations.

Ezzamel, M. & Willmott, H. (1998). Accounting for teamwork: a critical study of group-based systems of organizational control. Administrative Science Quarterly, 43, 358-396.

Fried, Y., & Ferris, G. R. (1987). The validity of the job characteristics model: A review and meta-analysis. Personnel Psychology, 40, 287-322/

Gladstein, D. L. (1984). Groups in context: A model of task group effectiveness. Administrative Science Quarterly, 29, 499-517.

Goodman, P. S. (1979). Assessing Organizational Change: the Rushton Quality of Work Experiment. New York: John Wiley.

Goodman, P., & Devadas, R., & Hughson, T. (1988). Groups and productivity: analysing the effectiveness of self-managing teams. In J. Campbell & R. Campbell (Eds.), Productivity in Organizations (pp. 295-327). San Francisco: Jossey –Bass.

Gospel, H., & Palmer, G. (1993). British Industrial Relations. London: Routledge.

Greller, M. M., Parsons, C. K., & Mitchell, D. R. D. (1992). Additive effects and beyond: Occupational stressors and social buffers in a police organisation. In J. C. Quick, L. R.

Murphy, & J. J. Hurrell (Eds.), Stress and Well-being at Work: Assessments and Interventions for Occupational Mental Health. American Psychological Association.

Griffin, R. W., Welsh, M. A., & Morehead, G. (1981). Perceived task characteristics and employee performance: A literature review. Academy of Management Review, 6, 655-664.

Guzzo, R.A., & Dickson, M. W. (1996). Teams in organizations: Recent research on performance and effectiveness. Annual Review of Psychology, 47, 307-338.

Guzzo, R. A., & Shea, G. P. (1992). Group performance and intergroup relations in organisations. In M. D. Dunnette & L. M. Hough (Eds.), Handbook of Industrial and Organizational Psychology, (Vol.2, pp. 271-326). Palo Alto, CA: Consulting Psychologists Press.

Hackman, J. R., & Oldham, G. R. (1975). Development of the job diagnostic survey. Journal of Applied Psychology, 60, 159-170.

Hackman, J. R., & Oldham, G. R. (1976). Motivation through the design of work: Test of a theory. Organizational Behavior and Human Performance, 15, 250-279.

Hackman, J. R., & Oldham, G. R. (1980). Work Redesign. Reading, MA: Addison-Wesley.

Hackman, J. R. (1977). Work design. In J. R. Hackman & J. L. Suttle (Eds.), Improving Life at Work. Santa Monica, CA: Goodyear Publishing Company Incorporated.

Hackman, J. R. (1987). The design of work teams. In J. W. Lorsch (Ed.), Handbook of Organizational Behavior (pp. 315-342). Englewood Cliffs, NJ: Prentice-Hall.

Hackman, J. R. (1990). Groups that Work (and those that don't): Creating Conditions for Effective Teamwork. San Francisco: Jossey Bass.

Hansen, O.N. & Rasmussen, K. (1995). Aendret arbejdsorganisering indenfor tekstilindustrien. En model til omlaegning af produktionen og til forebyggelse af arbejdsskader hos syersker. / Altered work structure in the textile industry: A model for reorganizing production systems and preventing occupational injuries among seamstresses. Nordisk Psykologi, 47(3), 197-212.

Heller, F., Pusic, E., Strauss, G., & Wilpert, B. (1998). Organisational Participation: Myth and Reality. New York: Oxford University Press.

Ilgen, D.R., Major, D.A., Hollenbeck, J.R., & Sego, D.J. (1993). Team research in the 1990s. In M.M. Chemers & R. Ayman (Eds.), Leadership Theory and Research: Perspectives and Directions (pp 245-270). San Diego, CA, USA: Academic Press Inc.

Jackson, P.R. & Martin, R. (1996). Impact of just-in-time on job content, employee attitudes, and well-being: A longitudinal analysis. Ergonomics, 39, 1-6.

Jackson, P. R., & Mullarkey, S. (2000). Lean production teams and health in garment manufacture. Journal of Occupational Health Psychology, 5, 231-245.

Jackson, P. R., Sprigg, C. A., & Parker, S. K. (2000). Interdependence as a key requirement for the successful introduction of teamworking: a case study. In S. Procter & F. Mueller (Eds.), Teamworking (pp. 83-102). Basingstoke: Macmillan Press.

Johnson, J.J., Hall, E.M., & Theorell, T. (1989). Combined effects of job strain and social isolation on cardiovascular disease morbidity and mortality in a random sample of Sweedish male working population. Scandinavian Journal of Work, Environment & Health, 15(4), 271-279.

Karasek, R. A., & Theorell, T. (1990). Healthy work: Stress, productivity, and the reconstruction of working life. New York: Basic Books.

Kirkman & Rosen (1997). A model of work team empowerment. In W.A. Pasmore & R.W. Woodman (Eds.), Research in Organizational Change and Development, vol 10: An annual Series Featuring Advances in Theory, Methodology and Research (pp 131-167). Greenwich, CT, USA: JAI Press Inc.

Kirkman & Shapiro (1997). The impact of cultural values on employees resistance to teams: Towards a model of globalized self-managing work team effectiveness. Academy of Management Review, 22(3), 730-757.

Klein, J. A. (1984). Why supervisors resist employee involvement. Harvard Business Review. September/October, pp. 87-95.

Kogler Hill, S.E. (1997). Team leadership theory. In P. Northouse (Ed.), Leadership: Theory and Practice. Sage Publications.

Kopelman, R. E. (1985). Job redesign and productivity: A review of the evidence. National Productivity Review, 4, 237-255.

Kristensen, T.S. (1996). Job stress and cardiovascular disease: A theoretical critical review. Journal of Occupational Health Psychology, 1(3), 246-260.

Landsbergis, P.A., Schnall, P.L., Warren, K. & Pickering, T.G. (1994). Association between ambulatory blood pressure and alternative formulations of job strain. Scadinavian Journal of Work, Environment and Health, 20(5), 349-363.

Landsbergis, P.A., Adler, P.S., Babson, S., Johnson, J., Kaminski, M., Lessin, N., MacDuffie, J.P., Nishiyama, K., Parker, S., & Richardson, C. (1998). Lean production and worker health: A discussion. New Solutions, 8, 499-523.

Letize, L., & Donovan, M. (1990). The supervisor's changing role in high involvement organizations. Journal of Quality and Participation, March, pp. 62-65.

Levine, D. I., & Tyson, L. D.A. (1990). Participation and productivity and the firm's environment. In A. S. Blinder (Ed.), Paying for productivity: A look at the evidence. Washington, D. C.: The Brookings Institution.

Liden, R. C., Wayne, S. J., & Bradway, L. K. (1997). Task interdependence as a moderator of the relation between group control and performance. Human Relation, 50, 169-181.

Macy, B. A., & Izumi, H. (1993). Organizational change, design, and work innovation: a meta-analysis of 131 North American field studies – 1961-1991. Research in Organizational Change and Design (Vol. 7). Greenwich, CT: JAI Press.

Manz, C. C., & Sims, H. P. (1987). Leading workers to lead themselves: the external leadership of self-managed work teams. Administrative Science Quarterly, 32, 106-128.

Manz, C. C., & Sims, H. (1993). Business Without Bosses: How Self Managing Teams are Building High Performance Companies. New York: Wiley.

Manz, C. C. (1992). Self-leading work teams – moving beyond self-management. Human Relations, 45, 1119-1140.

Marchington, M. (2000). Teamworking and employee involvement: terminology, evaluation and context. In S. Procter & F. Mueller (Eds.), Teamworking (pp. 60-80). Basingstoke: Macmillan Press.

Moch, M. K. (1980). Job involvement, internal motivation, and employees' integration into networks of work relationships. Organisational Behavior and Human Performance, 25, 15-31.

Mohrman, S. A., & Cohen, S. G. (1995). When people get out of the box: New relationships, new systems. In A. Howard (Ed.), The Changing Nature of Work (pp.365-410). San Francisco: Jossey-Bass.

Mohrman, S.A., Cohen, S. G., & Mohrman, A. M. (1995). Designing Team-Based Organizations. San Francisco: Jossey-Bass.

Morgeson, F.P., Aiman-Smith, L.D., & Campion, M.A. (1997). Implementing work teams: Recommendations from organizational behavior and development. In M.M. Beyerlin &

D.A. Johnson (Eds.), Advances in Interdisciplinary Studies of Work Teams, Vol 4 (pp 1-44). Greenwich, CI, USA: JAI Press Inc.

Mueller, F. (1994). Teams between hierarchy and commitment: change strategies and the 'internal environment'. Journal of Management Studies, 31, 383-403.

Mueller, F., Proctor, S., & Buchanan, D. (2000). Team working in its context(s): Antecedents, nature and dimensions. Human Relations, 3 (11), 1387 to 1424.

Mullarkey, S., Jackson, P. R., & Parker, S. K. (1995). Employee reactions to JIT manufacturing practices: A two-phase investigation. International Journal of Operations and Production Management, 15, 62-81.

Murakami, T. (1997). The autonomy of teams in the car industry – a cross national comparison. Work Employment and Society, 11, 749-758.

Osburn, J. D., Moran, L., Musselwhite, E., & Zenger, J. H. (1990). Self Directed Work Teams: The New American Challenge. New York: Irwin.

Osterman, P. (1994). How common is workplace transformation and who adopts it? Industrial and Labor Relations Review. Vol. 47, No. 2 (January), pp. 173-188.

Parker, S. K., & Axtell, C. M. (in press). Seeing another point of view: Antecedents and outcomes of employee perspective taking. Academy of Management Journal.

Parker, S. K., & Sprigg, C. A. (1999). Minimizing strain and maximizing learning: The role of job demands, job control, and proactive personality. Journal of Applied Psychology, 84, 925-993.

Parker, S. K., & Wall, T. D. (1998). Job and Work Design: Organizing Work To Promote Well-Being and Effectiveness. London: Sage.

Parker, S. K. & Whybrow, A. (1998). A changing work place: Mental health consequences of flexible working. In McCaig, R. and M. Harrington (Eds.) The Changing Nature of Occupational Health. HSE Books: Norwich, UK. ISBN 0-7176-1665-7.

Parker, S. K. (1998). Role breadth self-efficacy: Relationship with work enrichment and other organizational practices. Journal of Applied Psychology, 83, 835-852.

Parker, S. K., & Wall, T. D. (1998). Job and Work Design: Organizing Work To Promote Well-Being and Effectiveness. London: Sage.

Parker, S. K., & Sprigg, C. A. (1999). Minimizing strain and maximizing learning: The role of job demands, job control, and proactive personality. Journal of Applied Psychology, 84, 925-993.

Parker, S. K., Jackson, P. R., Sprigg, C.A., and Whybrow, A.C. (1998) Organizational interventions to reduce the impact of poor work design. CRR 196/1998. HSE Books: Norwich, UK.

Parkes, K.R., & Sparkes, T.J. (1998). Organizational interventions to reduce stress: Are they effective? A review of the literature? CRR 193/1998. HSE Books: Norwich, UK.

Pasmore, W.A. (1978). The comparative impacts of sociotechnical system, job redesign and survey-feedback interventions. In W.A. Pasmore & J. Sherwood (Eds.), Sociotechnical Systems: a Source Book. San Diego: University Associates.

Pasmore, W. A. (1988). Designing Effective Organizations: The Sociotechnical Systems Perspective. John Wiley & Sons: Toronto.

Pearce, J. A., & Ravlin, E. C. (1987). The design and activation of self-regulating work groups. Human Relations, 40(11), 751-782.

Pearson, C. A. L. (1992). Autonomous workgroups: An evaluation at an industrial site. Human Relations, 45(9), 905-936.

Procter, S., & Mueller, F. (2000). Teamworking: strategy, structure, systems and culture. In S. Procter & F. Mueller (Eds.), Teamworking (pp. 3-24). Basingstoke: Macmillan Press.

Rice, A. K. (1958). Productivity and Social Organization. London: Tavistock.

Schnall, P.L., Schwartz, J.E., Landsbergis, P.A., Warren, K. & Pickering, T.G. (1998). A longitudinal study of job strain and ambulatory blood pressure: Results from a three-year follow-up. Psychometric Medicine, 60, 697-706.

Schnall, P.L., Landsbergis, P.A., & Baker, D. (1994). Job strain and cardiovascular disease. Annual Review of Public Health, 15, 381-411.

Simpson, N. (2002). The effects of new ways of working on employees' stress levels. CRR 259/2000. HSE Books: Norwich, UK.

Smith, A.P., Wadsworth, E., Johal, S.S., Davey Smith, G. & Peters, T. (2000). The scale of occupational stress: The Bristol stress and health at work study. CRR 265/2000. HSE Books: Norwich, UK.

Spector, P. E., & O'Connell, B. J. (1994). The contribution of personality traits, negative affectivity, locus of control and type A as to the subsequent reports of job stressors and job strains. Journal of Occupational and Organisational Psychology, 67, 1-11.

Sprigg, C. A., Jackson, P. R., & Parker, S. K. (2000). Production team-working: The importance of interdependence for employee strain and satisfaction. Human Relations, 53, 1519-1543.

Stansfield, S., Head, J. & Marmot, M. (2000). Work related factors and ill health the Whitehall II Study. CRR 266/2000. HSE Books: Norwich, UK.

Stewart, G.L. (2000). Meta-analysis of Wok Teams Research Published between 1977 and 1998. Paper presented at Academy of Management Conference, Toronto, Canada.

Sundstrom, E., De Meuse, K. P., & Futrell, D. (1990). Work teams: Applications and effectiveness. American Psychologist, 45(2), 120-133.

Susman, G.I. (1976). Autonomy at Work: A Sociotechnical analysis of Participative Management. New York: Praeger.

Tannenbaum, S.I., Salas, E., & Cannon-Bowers, J.A (1996). Promoting team effectiveness. In M.A West (Ed.), Handbook of Work Group Psychology (pp. 503-530). New York: John Wiley.

Tesluk, P.E., & Mathieu, J.E. (1999). Overcoming road blocks to effectiveness: Incorporating management of performance barriers into models of work group effectiveness. Journal of Applied Psychology, 84(2), 200-217.

Trist, E. L., & Bamforth, K. W. (1951). Some social and psychological consequences of the long-wall method of coal-getting. Human Relations, 4, 3.38.

Turnbull, P.J. (1988). The limits to "Japanisation": Just-in-time, labour relations and the UK automotive industry. New Technology, Work and Employment, 3, 7-20.

Ulleberg, P. & Rundmo, T. (1997). Job stress, social support, job satisfaction and absenteeism among offshore oil personnel. Work and Stress, 11(3), 215-228.

Wall, T. D., & Clegg, C. W. (1981). A longitudinal field study of group work redesign. Journal of Occupational Behaviour, 2, 31-49.

Wall, T. D., & Jackson, P. R. (1995). New manufacturing initiatives and shopfloor work design. In A. Howard (Ed.), The changing nature of work (pp.139-174). San Francisco: Jossey-Bass.

Wall, T. D., Kemp, N. J. Jackson, P. R. J., & Clegg, C. W. (1986). Outcomes of autonomous work groups: A long-term field experiment. Academy of Management Journal, 29(2), 280-304.

Walton, R. E., & Schlesinger, L. A. (1979). Do supervisors thrive in participative work systems? Organizational Dynamics, 8, 24-39.

Walton, R. E. (1977). Work innovations at Topeka: after six years. The Journal of Applied Behavioral Science, 13(3), 422-433.

Warr, P. B. (1990). Decision latitude, job demands, and employee well-being. Work and Stress, 4, 285-294.

Waterson, P. E., Clegg, C. W., Bolden, R., Pepper, K., Warr, P. B., & Wall, T. D. (1997). The use and effectiveness of modern manufacturing practices in the United Kingdom. Unpublished report for the ESRC Centre for Organisation and Innovation, Institute of Work Psychology, University of Sheffield, England.

Weldon, E. & Weingart, L.R. (1993). Group goals and group performance. British Journal of Social Psychology, 32(4), 307-334.

Wellins, R. S., Byham, W. C., & Wilson, J. M. (1991). Empowered teams: Creating self-directed work groups that improve quality, productivity, and participation. Jossey-Bass Publishers: San Francisco.

West, M. A., & Patterson, M. G. (1998, January, 8). Profitable personnel. People Management, 4(2), 27-31.

West, M. A., Borrill, C. S., & Unsworth, K. (1998). Team effectiveness in organizations. In C. L. Cooper & I. T. Robinson (Eds.). International review of industrial and organizational psychology, Vol. 13 (pp. 1-48). Chichester: Wiley.

Whybrow, A., & Parker, S. K. (2000). Introducing teamworking: managing the process of change. In S. Procter & F. Mueller (Eds.), Teamworking (pp. 103-124). Basingstoke: Macmillan Press.

Womack, J. P., Jones, D. T., & Roos, D. (1990). The Machine that Changed the World. New York: Rawson Associates.

Wright, T. A., Bonett, D. G., & Sweeney, D. A. (1993). Mental health and work performance: Results of a longitudinal field study. Journal of Occupational and Organizational Psychology, 66, 277-284.

Wright, B. M, & Cordery, J. L. (1999). Production uncertainty as a contextual moderator of employee reactions to job design. Journal of Applied Psychology, 84, 456-463.

GLOSSARY

Advanced Manufacturing Technology (AMT)

Computer-based technologies, such as those used to control machine operation (robots, computer numerically controlled machine tools) or material handling. AMT's major advantage lies in computer control, such as allowing machines to be switched from making one product to another by loading software rather than physically re-setting machines.

Autonomous work groups

See *self-managed teams.*

Autonomy *(see also job autonomy)*

The discretion to make decisions and decide how and when tasks are done. Jobs often differ in the level of autonomy they have, or the extent to which employees are able to make their own decisions (e.g., without referring to a supervisor).

Business Process Engineering (BPR)

The redefinition of business organisation, systems and practices around those central to the goals of the customer and the organisation.

Cellular manufacturing

The grouping of machines, people, and processes into 'cells' where a particular product or type of product is made.

Context *(also referred to as organisational context)*

Refers to aspects of the organisational environment in which the team or individual operates (e.g., task interdependence, organisational culture, organisational structure, technology used, etc.).

Contingency

A factor that affects, or moderates, the relationship between two aspects. For example, interdependence is usually considered a contingency factor that affects the relationship between team working and outcomes. Thus, positive outcomes of team working are expected if interdependence is high but positive outcomes are less likely if task interdependence is low.

Continuous improvement (CI)

The philosophy and practice of continuously improving the work environment and work practices, usually in a step-by-step incremental way, to bring about improvements in individual and organisational performance.

Control group / Comparison group

A group that does not experience the same intervention as the group of interest, thus allowing the researcher to better understand the cause of change in the intervention group.

Cross sectional research design

A research design where information is gathered at a single point in time. This contrasts to longitudinal research designs *(see data).*

Data

Information gathered for the purpose of research. See *qualitative data* and *quantitative data.*

Delayering

Removing layers of management, which has the effect of reducing the hierarchy within an organisation. Usually accompanies empowerment and other forms of work redesign.

Deskilling

See *job simplification.*

Downsizing

The purposeful reduction in the size of the labour force with the aim of achieving gains of productivity.

Empowerment

A form of work design that involves providing front-line employees with 'power' over their jobs and work environment, including the knowledge, skill and information to make use of the greater control. See also *job enrichment* and *job redesign.*

Flexible forms of work organisation (or flexible working)

Organising and managing work to enhance flexibility and speed of response, such as through multiskilling, flexible work teams and self-managed teams.

Flexible work teams

Teams in which team members are multiskilled and able to help each other carry out their tasks.

Flexible working

See *flexible forms of work organisation.*

Horizontal job enlargement

See *job enlargement.*

Improvement groups (See also *total quality management).*

Groups of volunteer employees who meet off the job to identify ways to improve their work processes using problem-solving techniques (often termed *quality circles, continuous improvement groups).*

Interdependence (See also *task interdependence)*

The extent to employees are dependent on others for the necessary information, materials and skills to perform their jobs effectively.

Interdependent tasks *(also called task or process interdependence)*

Tasks that are linked together such that performing one task affects, or is affected by, the next task. Ideally, if the level of task interdependence is high, jobs should be structured so that employees engaged in them can co-operate and co-ordinate their efforts. Team working is often appropriate for highly interdependent tasks.

Job autonomy *(also called autonomy, job control)*

The level of autonomy, or discretion, present in a job (e.g., the extent to which an employee can control the timing and methods of their work).

Job characteristics *(see also work design characteristics)*

A term to describe relatively objective aspects of jobs that can affect employee attitudes and behaviour. Important job characteristics include: job autonomy, task variety, task identity, task significance, and job feedback.

Job control

See *job autonomy.*

Job design *(also called work design)*

Refers to the way in which work tasks are organised and managed, such as the level of job autonomy that employees have and their level of task variety.

Job enlargement (also called *horizontal job enlargement)*

A form of work redesign that involves expanding jobs so that they include a greater number and range of activities (e.g., doing filing, mail-sorting and word processing activities rather than just one of these).

Job enrichment (see also *empowerment)*

A form of work redesign that involves restructuring work (usually at the individual level) to increase responsibility for decisions traditionally made by a supervisor (e.g., decisions about work schedules), or allowing employees to take on extra skilled tasks (e.g., production employees undertake basic maintenance activities or order supplies).

Job redesign

See *empowerment, job enrichment, and self-managed teams.*

Job rotation

A form of work redesign that involves employees moving at regular intervals to perform different tasks.

Job satisfaction

A positive affective reaction to the job. Thus a person with high job satisfaction feels mostly positive about their job content.

Job simplification (also called *deskilling)*

The design of jobs based on principles of scientific management and simplification (e.g., breaking jobs down into their smallest parts and allocating one part to each employee).

Job strain

See *work related stress; well-being.*

Just-in-time (JIT)

A production system whereby the product undergoes one part of the process of manufacture 'just-in-time' to be 'pulled' to the next process, eventually being delivered 'just-in-time' to the customer. Generally introduced to reduce work-in-progress and levels of inventory.

Lean production

An approach to production, which has as a core principle 'doing more with less', and its central focus is on the removal of inventory from different stages of the production process. Key elements of lean production include simplifying work processes, employees working interdependently to keep the process going, and tightly-linked work flows.

Lean production teams

Teams which work under a lean production ethos. The teams usually have standard operating procedures that regulate their work, and are typically managed by first-line supervisors. Team members often carry out off-line improvement activities.

Longitudinal research design

Gathering information at more than one point in time, typically from the same people. To assess the effect of interventions, information is usually gathered before the change and after the change.

Mental health

See *well-being, and work-related stress.*

Mental health risks

See *psychosocial risks.*

Multiskilling

Increasing employees' skill base so that they can carry out multiple tasks.

Organisational context

See *context.*

Participation

A general term used to indicate employee involvement in decision making, although it is often specifically applied to the process of involving employees in introducing change (such as work redesign, introducing new technologies).

Process interdependence

See *interdependent tasks.*

Production uncertainty *(see also uncertainty)*

The extent to which technology and production process are variable and unpredictable, such as how often machines need to be continually adjusted to keep them within required tolerances, how frequently new products are introduced, and the extent of variation in raw material specification.

Psychological health

See *well-being.*

Psychosocial risks (also called *mental health risks)*

Aspects of job content, work organisation and management, and of environmental, social and organisational conditions that might have the potential for psychological and physical harm.

Qualitative data

Information which is generally non-numerical, often collected through observing situations or people, through individual interviews, and/or group discussions. Such data may be collected using tape recorders or written notes.

Quality circles

See *improvement groups.*

Quantitative data

Information which is numerical, generally collected using questionnaires. Also, numerical data can come from company records, such as number of accidents and performance figures. Qualitative material can be converted into quantitative data, such as by counting the number of references to a specific theme in interviews.

Role clarity

Having a clear sense of what is required and expected, such as being clear what the goals of the job are and how those goals should be achieved.

Role conflict

Having consistent expectations.

Self-managed teams (see *autonomous work groups).*

Team that have autonomy over day-to-day operational decisions (e.g., deciding who does what, when, how) as well as input into the running of the group (e.g., selection of team members). Also referred to as *autonomous work groups, semi-autonomous work groups, self-directed teams, self-leading teams.* Note that introducing self-managing teams differs from job enrichment in that it involves redesigning the work of groups of employees.

Single status

Efforts by the organisation to remove or reduce the traditional indicators of higher employment status within the organisation. Manifestations include employees at all levels (including managers) having the same car park, wearing the same uniform, eating in the same dining room. The premise can be extended to include job terms and conditions (e.g., all employees having access to shares, etc.).

Skill variety *(see also work design characteristics)*

A job that has a varied range of tasks and that utilises a range of the employee's skills.

Sociotechnical systems approach (See *autonomous work groups)*

An approach originating from the Tavistock Institute of Human Relations during the 1950s, the basic principle being that there should be joint optimisation and parallel design of social subsystems (people, aspects, roles, etc.) and technical subsystems (machinery, etc.) in organisations. Applied to the level of jobs, this approach led to the development of autonomous work groups.

Strain
See *work-related stress.*

Task
See *interdependent tasks.*

Task identity
Doing a 'whole' piece of work rather than a fragment (e.g., helping to assemble a whole car rather than assembling only the wheel).

Task interdependence
See *interdependence.*

Task significance
Doing work that feels important and meaningful.

Team
A group of individuals with a defined organisational function and identity, shared objectives and goals, and interdependent roles.

Team effectiveness
The extent to which the team is performing well, has satisfied members, and is sustainable.

Team performance
How well the team is doing on criteria relevant to the organisation. In production organisations, team performance measures usually include aspects such as productivity, quality and cost effectiveness of the team.

Team viability
A team's ability to continue to work together.

Total Quality Management (TQM)
A strategy where quality is no longer seen as a policing and rectification function (e.g., quality inspection), but as an integral part of the management systems. Many methods and practices are

used, such as forming quality circles (see *improvement groups*), changing product designs to improve manufacturability, and involving employees in fault prevention and rectification.

Traditional work groups

Groups of employees who are controlled and managed by a first line supervisor. Traditional work groups are also usually not very flexible, with most employees carrying out a single task.

Uncertainty *(also called product uncertainty)*

Uncertain production processes are complex with high information-processing requirements (e.g., when there are large numbers of products and frequent changes in product design). For example, making customised control systems is likely to involve much greater uncertainty and complexity than the mass production of dishwashing liquid.

Well-being *(also called psychological health; see also work-related stress)*

Refers to the general mental health of an employee. Work-related well-being is often measured by aspects such as job satisfaction, organisational commitment and work-related stress.

Work design *(also called job design)*

The way that roles and responsibilities are organised and distributed amongst employees, such as the extent to which employees are authorised to make their own decisions and the degree of variety in their jobs. See also *empowerment, work design characteristics, job enrichment, job simplification, autonomous work groups.*

Work design characteristics

Key features of jobs. Hackman and Oldham (1980) identified five core job characteristics that affect employees' motivation and performance:

- Autonomy, or job control (the extent to which the job allows jobholders to exercise choice and discretion in their work)
- Feedback from the job (the extent to which the job itself provides job holders with information on their performance)
- Task identity (the extent to which the job involves completing a whole identifiable piece of work)
- Task significance (the extent to which the job has an impact inside or outside the organisation)
- Skill variety (the degree to which the job requires different skills)

However, other work design characteristics have also been identified (e.g., role conflict).

Work redesign

Re-structuring work to change the way that roles and tasks are organised and distributed. The term is usually used to indicate moving away from simplified jobs towards more enriched and autonomous work roles. For specific examples, see *empowerment, job enrichment, job enlargement, job rotation, self-managed teams.*

Work-related stress

The negative strain consequences associated with work (also called 'job strain'), such as feeling anxious or feeling depressed as a result of work. The term 'employee well-being' and 'employee mental health' are more general terms, encompassing work-related stress as well as outcomes such as job satisfaction and general psychological health.

Printed and published by the Health and Safety Executive

C3 11/01